HARRY DOWNIE

A MAN AND HIS MISSION

*How one man's devotion to the
California Missions resurrected them
after their tragic downfall.*

— John Billman —

Harry Downie
A memoir by John Billman

Copyright © 2022 by John Billman

All rights reserved. No part of this publication may be reproduced, distributed, or transmitted in any form or by any means, including photocopying, recording, or other electronic or mechanical methods, without the prior written permission of the publisher, except in the case of brief quotations embodied in critical reviews and certain other noncommercial uses permitted by copyright law. For permission requests, write to the publisher, addressed "Attention: Permissions Coordinator," at the address below.

Timewalker Press
P.O. Box 1434
Salinas, California, 93902

Printed in the United States of America

Publisher's Cataloging-in-Publication Data
Andresen, Peter Garth

ISBN: 978-0-9854285-8-7 (paperback)

Cover portrait of Harry Downie. Painted by Frank Ambrosio. Courtesy of Carmel Mission Basilica Museum and the Rev. Paul P. Murphy.

*To my wife, Dolores,
my beloved Pyooch*

Contents

Highlights of the Life and Times of Harry Downie	vii
Preface	xiii
Introduction	xvii
Chapter 1: A Forty-Nine-Year Visit	1
Chapter 2: Boyhood Memories	6
Chapter 3: A One-Man Crew	11
Chapter 4: A Note in a Bottle	20
Chapter 5: Mission San Carlos Borromeo	24
Chapter 6: The Birthplace of California	29
Chapter 7: Our Lady of Bethlehem	34
Chapter 8: Captain of the Indians	38
Chapter 9: A Year of Earthquakes	41
Chapter 10: The Founder of California	46
Chapter 11: A Papal Visit	52
Chapter 12: A Steak in the Freezer	59
Chapter 13: Secularization	67
Chapter 14: Restorations	71
Chapter 15: An American da Vinci	83
Chapter 16: A Remarkable Man	102

Epilogue: The Missions in the Order of Their Founding	109
Notes	123
Bibliography	141
Published Sources	143
Periodicals and Letters	149
Index	157

HIGHLIGHTS OF THE LIFE AND TIMES OF HARRY DOWNIE

• **1903** Henry John Downie is born in San Francisco on August 25. He will always be known as Harry.	• **1903** Orville and Wilbur Wright conduct the first powered flight near Kitty Hawk, North Carolina, on December 17.
• **1906** An earthquake in San Francisco on April 18 knocks the Downie home off its foundation and onto the street.	• **1906** San Francisco is destroyed by an earthquake and fire on April 18–19. Six hundred people die, and thousands are left homeless.
• **1918** Harry installs a tile roof on Mission Dolores in San Francisco. He is fifteen years old.	• **1918** The Great Influenza pandemic, the deadliest outbreak in history, takes a half million American lives.
• **1929** A fire destroys Mission Santa Clara in 1926. Harry restores the main altar and carves new statues and is a consultant for the rebuilding of the mission, which is completed in 1929.	• **1929** The stock market crash on "Black Tuesday," October 29, ushers in the Great Depression.

- **1931**
Harry arrives at Mission San Carlos Borromeo in Carmel on August 28 for a visit, but he stays there for the rest of his life.
- **1936**
Harry marries Mabel McEldowney of Carmel, at Mission San Carlos Borromeo, on April 18.
- **1939**
Harry discovers the exact location of the cross Father Junipero Serra erected on the Carmel Mission courtyard on August 24, 1771.
- **1943**
Harry supervises the opening of Father Junipero Serra's grave in August, for canonization proceedings.
- **1944**
Harry erects a cross on Carmel beach on the 175th anniversary of the raising of the cross there by the Portola-Crespi expedition on December 10, 1769.

- **1931**
The Empire State Building, then the tallest building in the world, opens in New York City.
- **1936**
Jesse Owens wins four gold medals at the "Nazi" Olympics in Berlin.
- **1939**
Pan Am Airlines begin the first regular trans-Atlantic passenger service.
- **1943**
General Dwight D. Eisenhower is named Supreme Commander of Allied forces in Europe.
- **1944**
The Allies invade Europe at Normandy on D-Day, June 6.

- **1945**
Harry builds Junipero Serra School on the grounds of Carmel Mission. It opens on September 10.

- **1948**
Harry is made a Knight Commander of Isabella La Catolica, by General Franco of Spain.

- **1954**
Harry is made a Knight of St. Gregory, by Pope Pius XII, for a lifetime of outstanding work on behalf of the church.

- **1961**
Carmel Mission Church is elevated to a minor basilica on April 27.

- **1969**
The belfry of Carmel Mission is reproduced on a six-cent postage stamp issued July 16, commemorating California's Bicentennial.

- **1945**
Germany surrenders on May 7, ending the war in Europe. Japan surrenders on August 14, ending World War II.

- **1948**
The United States recognizes the new state of Israel on May 14 and admits 205,000 refugees from Europe.

- **1954**
The Supreme Court orders school desegregation in *Brown v. Board of Education* on May 17.

- **1961**
Commander Alan B. Shepard, Jr., U.S. Navy, is the first American in space on the Mercury rocket, on May 5.

- **1969**
Neil Armstrong and Buzz Aldrin of Apollo XI are the first men to walk on the Moon on July 20.

Harry erects a cross on Monterey beach on December 9, amid celebration by local dignitaries, to commemorate the 200th anniversary of the placing of the cross there by the Portola-Crespi expedition, which resulted in the founding of Monterey.

- **1972**

August 25 is "Harry Downie Day" at Carmel Mission Basilica. Harry's 69th birthday is celebrated with a Mass said by Bishop Harry A. Clinch, a testimonial dinner and presentation of a bronze plaque honoring his forty-one years of restoring Carmel Mission.

- **1976**

Harry is named a Knight of Castle Belvere, by King Juan Carlos of Spain, for his work in making the Spanish influence known.

- **1972**

Five men are arrested for breaking into the Democratic National Committee headquarters at the Watergate complex in Washington, D.C., on June 17. A federal grand jury indicts five burglars and two former White House aides in a trial on September 15.

- **1976**

The Bicentennial of the United States is celebrated coast to coast.

• 1980

Harry dies on March 10 and is buried in the Carmel Mission cemetery. Congressman Leon Panetta addresses the House of Representatives in the nation's capital on July 1, on the subject "Harry Downie, Bringing History to Life."

The Sir Harry Downie Museum is dedicated on August 25.

• 1980

Mount St. Helens in Washington state erupts on May 18, demolishing a 230-square-mile area, reducing the size of the mountain by 1,300 feet in a matter of seconds and killing fifty-seven people.

Preface

Immortality is not a gift,
Immortality is an achievement;
and only those who strive
mightily shall possess it.

—Edgar Lee Masters
American poet

Harry Downie's life was centered on his family and on the California Missions. Carmel Mission was his favorite. Harry had an encyclopedic knowledge of the missions and of the padres and soldiers who established them. In restoring the California Missions, Harry became part of California history. He became part of my history as well. Some of my fondest boyhood memories are of going to Harry and Mabel's house for dinner with my parents. After dinner, Harry, a proud San Franciscan, and my father, a proud Bostonian, would seat themselves at opposite ends of the dinner table Harry had made when he built his house, and then have a drink and argue about the relative merits of California and New England. About that time, Harry would send me to his library behind his house, where I would immerse myself in his collection of books, paintings and mission artifacts. Almost seventy years later, I can still visualize Harry with a gleam in his eye, his gold tooth shining, barely able to suppress a smile.

Harry was my godfather, but I could not have written his story without the aid of his daughter Miriam. Miriam shared anecdotes and information about Harry with me as we sat at the same table again, in her house. She talked of co-authoring this book with me, but she was ill, and as her illness progressed, she turned the writing over to me, confident of my ability to write it. I will always be grateful to her. Harry's story needed to be told, and I am honored to have written it.

At Harry's funeral on March 13, 1980, at his beloved Carmel Mission Basilica, I repeated the words to Miriam of Edwin M. Stanton, Abraham Lincoln's Secretary of War, upon Lincoln's death: "Now he belongs to the ages."

Miriam died on January 22, 2009. I hope she is looking down on me with approval.

Miriam Downie

1940–2009

Harry Downie

Harry Downie, 1936
Courtesy Monterey Diocese Archives

INTRODUCTION

The California Missions pioneered an agricultural and commercial industry that flourished for almost sixty-five years, was the foundation of California's history and culture, and was the sole industry in Alta California. Mission-style architecture, with its stucco exteriors, red tile roofs, and porticoes, has exerted a powerful influence on California's residential, commercial and public buildings, notably in the city of Santa Barbara and on the campus of Stanford University. The Burlingame railroad station, built in 1894, used roof tiles from Mission San Antonio de Padua. It was the first public building designed in mission-style architecture.

President George W. Bush recognized the historic role of the missions when he signed HR 1446, the "California Mission Preservation Act," into law on November 30, 2004, providing $10 million over a five-year period to the California Missions Foundation for projects related to restoration of the missions. The Foundation is a volunteer, tax-exempt organization established to preserve the California Missions.

Through the efforts of groups such as the Foundation, and of Harry Downie, who devoted his life to the restoration of the missions, the mission period of California history has been revived and preserved for future generations, and immortalized in the names of cities and towns from San Diego to San Francisco.

Father Ramon Mestres, pastor of San Carlos Church in Monterey from 1893 until his death in 1930, standing in the remains of Father Junipero Serra's cell at Mission San Carlos Borromeo in 1926. A white cross marks the cell. When the buildings were in ruins, a cross marked Father Serra's cell because he died there.

Courtesy California History Room & Archives, Monterey Public Library

*If you would not be forgotten, as soon as you are dead and rotten,
either write things worth reading, or do things worth the writing.*
—Benjamin Franklin
Poor Richard's Almanac

CHAPTER 1

A FORTY-NINE-YEAR VISIT

*There is a strange
charm in the thoughts
of a good legacy...*

—Miguel de Cervantes
Don Quixote

Harry Downie has left us a rich legacy in the California Missions. Harry devoted his life to the missions, restoring them to their former grandeur, and in the process, becoming a part of California history.

Harry Downie was an unpretentious man, a stout fellow who walked about the grounds of Carmel Mission with an unlit cigar clamped between his teeth, and with his faithful dog, Gaspar, at his side.

In his battered felt hat and his work-stained clothing, Harry looked like an ordinary workman, but he was the curator of Carmel Mission, he restored the mission from an abandoned ruin to an architectural award-winning basilica,[1] and he built an elementary school on the site of the former Indian dormitories—and he did this almost single-handedly.

Harry arrived at Carmel Mission on August 28, 1931, the 147th anniversary of the death of Father Junipero (hoo-neep'-ah-ro) Serra, founder of the mission. Little remained besides the sandstone-and-mortar church standing like a sentinel amid mounds of waist-high adobe ruins. The winds had blown sand and dirt in through the open doors and windows, and tall weeds were growing inside the church. The tile roof had collapsed in 1852, and people had helped themselves to bricks, tile and timbers.[2]

Father Angelo Casanova, pastor of San Carlos Church in Monterey, replaced the roof in 1884 for the centennial of Father Serra's death. Jane Stanford, co-founder with her husband, Leland Stanford, of Stanford University, was a major financial contributor of the project.[3] It was a shingle roof seventeen feet higher than the original roof and had a steep pitch.

When Helen Hunt Jackson, the nineteenth-century author and Native American rights advocate, saw the remains of the mission, she wrote, "It is a disgrace to both the Catholic Church and the state of California that this grand old ruin with its sepulchers, should be left to crumble away. If nothing is done to protect it, one short hundred years more will see it as a shapeless, wind-swept mound of sand."[4]

When Walter Colton, Monterey's first American alcalde (mayor), visited the mission, he wrote in his diary, "Only the church remains. I found the only being in it a great white owl who seemed to mourn its fall."[5]

When Robert Louis Stevenson visited the mission on San Carlos Day in 1879, he described it as "a ruined mission . . . there is no one left to care for the converted savage. The church is roofless . . . an antiquity in this new land."[6] San Carlos Day was November 4, the anniversary of the death of San Carlos Borromeo, patron saint of the mission. It was celebrated with Mass, and a barbecue and entertainment, even when the mission was abandoned. It was a social event as well as a religious celebration. The festival was alternately discontinued and revived, but renewed in 1964, and has been an annual event since then, although it is no longer held on November 4.

In his book *Across the Plains*, Stevenson described the sight of the Indians assembled amidst the ruins to hear Mass in the "little sacristy which is the only covered portion of the church. An aged Indian, stone-blind and about 80 years of age, conducts the singing; other Indians compose the choir . . . and pronounce the Latin so correctly that I could follow the meaning as they sang. . . . I have never seen faces more vividly lit up with joy than the faces of these Indian singers . . . and there among a crowd . . . you may hear God served with perhaps more touching circumstances than in any other temple under heaven."[7] In *The Monterey Californian*, Stevenson wrote, "A fine old church, a fine old race, both brutally neglected; a survival, a memory and a ruin. The United States Mint can coin many million more dollar pieces, but not make a single Indian; and when Carmel Church is in the dust, not all the wealth of all the states and territories can replace what has been lost." In an almost prophetic reference to Harry Downie, he wrote, "The managers of our hotels, or their successors, may have cause to bless the man who put a roof on Carmel Church."[8]

More than 200,000 people visit the mission each year.[9] President and Mrs. John F. Kennedy visited in 1960. Konrad Adenauer, former West German Chancellor, has toured the mission, and so has Stewart L. Udall, former U.S. Secretary of the Interior. Harry met Princess Margaret of the United Kingdom at the mission, and he was thrilled when she petted his dog Gaspar.[10] When former first lady Mrs. Lady Bird Johnson signed the guest register at the mission in 1966, she wrote, "It is a privilege to see this enchanting spot of history!"[11] President Dwight Eisenhower beamed when he saw Harry, and he extended his hand to him and said, "Oh I've heard of Mr. Downie. I did a painting of the mission once and it hangs in my office."[12] Pope John Paul II celebrated Mass at the mission in 1987.

Harry was a journeyman cabinetmaker, and before going to the mission he sailed around the world for four months as a ship's carpenter on the Dollar Steamship Line, remodeling and redecorating the ship's cabins and making repairs as needed. He saw some of the world, and he learned to empathize with the underprivileged.[13]

When he returned, he entered the Jesuit Novitiate in Los Gatos as a brother, but soon afterward he secured a cabinetmaker's job in Santa Barbara. "I carved better than I prayed, so the Lord told me to get busy and fix up his missions," Harry observed.[14] Lawrence Farrell, a boyhood friend of Harry from Monterey and a seminarian, was on his way to the

University of Fribourg in Switzerland to study. He went to Los Gatos to say goodbye to Harry. Harry told Lawrence of his plan to leave, and he gave him a letter to send to a cabinet-making firm in Santa Barbara. Lawrence kept the letter, and he called Harry the next day and told him it would be better to go to Monterey and spend some time at the mission.[15] Harry arrived at San Carlos Church in Monterey on August 27, 1931, and stayed at the rectory. The pastor, Msgr. Philip Scher, knowing that Harry had restored the altar and carved new statues at Mission Santa Clara after a fire destroyed it, asked Harry whether he could repair some of the old statues at Mission San Carlos Borromeo. Harry went to the mission the next day, and he took charge temporarily because Father Michael Murphy, the guardian, was not well. Harry took over the gardening and made repairs, but he kept seeing more work that needed to be done. Years later, he recalled, "I came for one month but I've been here for thirty-five years."[16] Harry spent the next forty-nine years of his life in Carmel.

CHAPTER 2

BOYHOOD MEMORIES

There is a divinity that shapes our ends, rough-hew them as we will.

—Shakespeare
Hamlet

Harry knew what he wanted to do from the time he was a boy—devote his life to the California Missions. He kept a scrapbook of the missions, and he made models of them.[17] He made a model of the façade of Carmel Mission when he was twelve years old. It is on display in the Sir Harry Downie Museum at Carmel Mission.

Harry admired Helen Hunt Jackson. He owned a first edition of her novel, *Ramona*, and he read it when he was a boy. His mother took him to see her house in Hemet, California, and he painted a picture of it, and he told his mother he wanted to build a house someday that looked like her house. When Harry built his house in Carmel in 1939, he built a Spanish-style adobe with a white stucco exterior and a red tile roof. He modeled the house after Helen Hunt Jackson's house, and he built his own furniture.[18]

"I was born and raised in the Mission Dolores parish in San Francisco, and my family too," Harry once reminisced, his brogue evoking the speech of his Scots Irish ancestors. "My people settled in the 1860s where Mission Dolores is now." Harry spent his youth working at Mission Dolores and taking care of the cemetery, the city's oldest burial ground, opened in 1776, the year the mission was established. Louis Antonio Arguello, the first governor of Alta California under Mexican rule, is buried there, as is Francisco de Haro, the first alcalde (mayor) of San Francisco.[19] The remaining graves date from the Gold Rush, including some who were hanged by the Committee of Vigilance, a citizens group formed in San Francisco in 1851 to stop robberies and other crimes, especially arson, which had become common and had gone unpunished by a weak city government. The Committee dwindled away after 100 days, but in 1856 another Committee of Vigilance was formed following the murders of two prominent citizens. On May 18, about 2,500 armed vigilantes took the offenders from jail, tried them and publicly hanged them four days later.[20]

Harry was born in San Francisco on August 25, 1903, to Henry John Downie and the former Rose Morrison.[21] Harry's father was a printer with Borgel and Downie Printers at 370 Second Street in San Francisco.[22] Harry was baptized at Mission Dolores on September 20, 1903. His baptismal name was Henry John Downie, but he was always Harry.[23] Two and a half years later, on Wednesday, April 18, 1906, at

5:12 a.m., a magnitude 8.3 earthquake rocked San Francisco like a cradle for twenty-eight seconds and set church bells ringing throughout the city.[24] It knocked the Downies' house off its foundation and onto the street. Harry's mother rescued him, but the casters on his bed rolled over her foot and broke her toes.[25] More than 600 people died in the earthquake and the fires that followed, and about 300,000 people were left homeless.[26] Distribution centers were set up to dole out food and supplies, but milk was available only to mothers with babies. People would hand a baby from one person to another so they could get milk. Two-year-old Harry was lent to all the neighbors.[27]

Mission Dolores acquired its name when Father Francisco Palou established it in 1776, in a brushwood shelter alongside Dolores Creek. Its true name is San Francisco de Asis, for Saint Francis of Assisi, founder of the Franciscan Order. Father Palou moved the mission to its present site and began construction on April 25, 1782. It was dedicated on April 3, 1791.[28] An estimated 36,000 adobe bricks were used in the construction. The church is twenty-two feet wide and 140 feet long. It is the oldest intact building in San Francisco.[29]

It was the parish church until 1876 when the new church was built alongside it to accommodate the expanding population of the city following the Gold Rush. Portions of the quadrangle were razed for the opening of 16th Street, and to make room for the new church. It was dedicated on the 100th anniversary of the mission's founding.

The 1906 earthquake spared Mission Dolores, but it damaged the new church so much that it had to be dismantled a few weeks later. A temporary wooden church served the parish until the ruined church was replaced in 1918 when it was dedicated at Christmas.[30] In 1916, when Father John Sullivan arrived as the pastor, he ordered the restoration of Mission Dolores. The original roof tiles were stored on the flat part of the roof of the new church. Harry carried them to the roof of Mission Dolores and replaced the tile roof by himself. He was fifteen years old.[31]

It was 1918, the year of the Great Influenza Epidemic, the deadliest outbreak in history. Almost everyone on earth was exposed to the disease and millions of people died. When it was over in 1919, half a million Americans would be dead.[32] Most cities banned public meetings, and public gathering places such as schools, churches and theatres were closed. The public was ordered to wear masks, and the police enforced the order. Harry wore a mask when he was working on the roof of the mission, but one day the wind was blowing, and it was dangerous walking across the planks, so he did not put on his mask. A policeman saw him and said, "Why don't you put on your mask? I'll put you under arrest if you don't put it on." "I didn't put it on," Harry recalled, "and he was waiting for me to come down at the front of the old mission, but I went onto the roof of the new church and went down through the tower and out on 16th Street and left him waiting there for me." Harry recalled the flu epidemic.

> Quite a number of people died, five in our block alone. They couldn't have regular funerals. The bodies were brought to the cemetery and left there for weeks. They

would put the bodies in a trench and put name plates on them and in a year the families could claim them and put them in their own plot in the cemetery. There was no Mass in any building in San Francisco. Mass was said in the streets. Everything was closed. It was like that for months.[33]

When Father Sullivan, Harry's mentor, recognized Harry's interest in everything about the mission, he persuaded him to learn the cabinetmaking trade. "I had other aspirations," Harry said, "but he knew me better than I knew myself."[34] Harry began his training as an apprentice cabinetmaker with the A. T. Hunt Cabinet firm in San Francisco on July 5, 1919. He completed his training in 1922. He used to go to Monterey on vacations and holidays and restore artifacts from Carmel Mission that were held at San Carlos Church in Monterey. Eventually, he placed them in a small museum in the rectory there.[35] As his reputation spread, he was called to work at the Flood, Crocker and Dollar estates in Pacific Heights in San Francisco and at the Hearst Castle.[36]

CHAPTER 3

A ONE-MAN CREW

*He was in love with
his work, and he felt
the enthusiasm for it
which nothing but the
work we can do well
inspires in us.*
—William Dean Howells
American author and editor

In 1932, Harry Downie began the restoration of Carmel Mission when he restored the former padres' library and an adjacent padres' cell as living quarters for himself. He lived in the room for over three years.[37] During the ensuing years, Harry supervised and directed every phase of the restoration of the mission. On Sundays, Harry left the Sunday comic strips in his room for Emilio Odello and Bruno Abluton, altar boys at both Masses, the 9 a.m. and the 11 a.m. Between Masses, the boys went to Harry's room and read the funnies.[38] Emilio Odello became an artichoke grower. His fields were a familiar sight on both sides of Highway 1 near Carmel Mission. Emilio's wife Bruna was a docent at the mission when there were no other docents. One evening, Emilio and Bruna invited Harry and friends of his from San Francisco, Earl and Margaret Currivan to dinner. Harry knew Emilio was squeamish, so he asked Earl about his mortuary business. Earl took the cue, and he went into graphic details of some of the morticians' procedures. Emilio was horrified and Harry was laughing, and soon everyone joined in the laughter. When an old white barn in the Odello fields was torn down, Emilio gave Harry some of the old-fashioned nails from it, and Harry used some of them when he moved Crespi Hall to its present location in 1951 to make way for the restoration of the west wing. Emilio and Harry, with his dog Gaspar, liked to sit on the portico of the mission, facing the courtyard and talk about old times. Occasionally, someone would ask them where they could find Harry Downie, because they would like to meet him. Harry would point his finger and say, "I think he went that way."[39]

Bruna Odello and the author at the Carmel Mission Festival

Photo by Dolores Billman

In 1932, Harry revived Father Serra's custom of removing the body of Christ from the crucifix on Good Friday. At the twelfth station of the cross, the sanctuary was darkened and lightning was simulated by turning the lights on and off, and thunder was simulated by a *matraca*, a board with nails driven into it with hinged hammers to hit the nails. At the 13th station of the cross, the body of Jesus was taken down from the cross. The arms dropped to the sides of the body, because the shoulders were set in leather sockets and they were jointed. A cloth about thirty-five feet long was placed under the arms and over the arms of the cross to hold the body up while the nails were removed. Two men would stand alongside the crucifix and hold the cloth until the body was down. Silence engulfed the church as the body was taken in solemn procession to the mortuary chapel where it lay in repose. The congregation left the church through the chapel so all could venerate the body. The custom was discontinued in 1972 because of the frail condition of the joints and hinges.[40]

On October 27, 1933, Mission San Carlos Borromeo became a parish, and the Rev. Michael O'Connell was named the first pastor.[41] Harry carved the Christ the King statue in the center of the church, across from the Mortuary Chapel, to commemorate the founding of the parish on the feast of Christ the King. The décor of the statue is changed with the liturgical season. In 1934, George Marion, a retired actor, wrote and directed a pageant titled The Apostle of California, for the 150th anniversary of the death of Father Junipero Serra on August

28, 1784. Father Serra was the founder of the mission and father-president of the California Missions. Harry built a rock wall and a stage and a 1,600-seat amphitheater for the pageant, which was presented nightly from August 24 through 28, 1934, against the backdrop of the bell tower. The California State Senate designated August 28, 1934, as Junipero Serra Day. In 1936, Harry used the lumber from the amphitheater to build a new ceiling for the church.[42] Harry said:

> The roof Father Casanova put on was 17 feet higher than the original. I had to remove the ceiling as well as the roof and then strip the church down to the original walls. The hardest part was to locate the exact angle of the original tile roof. Once I got that right I connected the supporting arches and installed them. Then I laid the new tile roof and plastered the new ceiling—so that Padre Lasuen might have supposed it was the original structure he built.[43]

In 1941, Harry completed the tourist entrance and he opened the gift shop.[44]

When "old Joe" McEldowney, a stonemason from Ireland was installing the floor in the church, he told Harry he wanted him to meet his daughter Mabel. Joe would take Harry to his house to meet Mabel, but Mabel would slip out the back door and go to the movies with a friend.

Harry and Mabel Downie at Carmel Mission
on their wedding day, April 18, 1936

Pat Hathaway Collection

One night, Harry and Joe waited outside the theatre. Harry met Mabel and they began dating, and on April 18, 1936, Father Murphy married them in Harry's room at the mission.[45] According to church law at that time, if one person was non-Catholic, the couple could not be married in the church sanctuary. Mabel was non-Catholic. One evening, during a dinner at Harry and Mabel's house, Monsignor James Culleton looked at Mabel and demanded, "Why aren't you a Catholic?" "No one ever asked me," Mabel replied. Harry was mortified. Standing behind Mabel, his face contorted, he gestured frantically for the Monsignor to be quiet. The next day, Monsignor John Ryan, also a dinner guest and the pastor of San Carlos Church in Monterey, went to Harry and Mabel's house for lunch; he brought a catechism and began giving Mabel lessons.[46] She had already been attending Mass and within a year, in 1958, she was baptized at the mission church. Harry and Mabel had two daughters; Miriam, born February 7, 1940, and Ann Marie, born October 31, 1945.[47]

When Miriam entered the Dominican convent in San Rafael, California, she was required to assume a religious name. The Reverend Mother suggested numerous saints' names to Harry, but Harry said, "you can take all those names and put them in a cannon and shoot them off." Then the Reverend Mother asked Harry what he thought of the name Sister Serra. Harry brightened and said, "oh yes—yes." Miriam was the first Sister Serra.[48]

Harry designed and landscaped the courtyard at the entrance to the church. Trees planted there in the 1920s grew so thick they concealed the view of the church, so Harry took them out, except for a pepper tree planted in 1922, and a cork tree planted about 1924, outside the present Sir Harry Downie Museum. Cork is made from the bark of the cork tree. The courtyard extended about twenty feet beyond the buildings to the road in front of the entrance. In the winter, rainwater rushed down the slope of the courtyard and accumulated at the front door of the church and the parishioners had to walk on planks to get inside, so Harry lowered the courtyard and installed a drainage system under the Jo Mora Chapel, which houses the Serra Memorial.[49]

In 1924, Jo Mora, an artist and sculptor, designed and sculpted the Serra Memorial. It depicts Father Junipero Serra in death, in the grieving presence of three other padres who are buried with him under the sanctuary floor of the church: Father Juan Crespi, Father Julian Lopez, and Father Fermin Lasuen,

Father Serra's lifelong friend who succeeded him as father-president of the mission system and who continued Father Serra's work building Mission San Carlos Borromeo.[50] Father Ramon Mestres, pastor of San Carlos Church in Monterey, commissioned Mora to build the memorial as a permanent monument to Father Serra. It is made of travertine marble and bronze and is mounted on a base eight feet wide and twelve feet long. It was to have been placed in the church where Father Serra is buried, but it was too large, so Father Mestres had a room built to accommodate it.[51] It is known as the Jo Mora Chapel. The memorial is usually referred to as a sarcophagus, but it is a cenotaph (sen uh taf), a monument erected in honor of a deceased person whose remains lie elsewhere. A sarcophagus is a stone coffin.

Sculptor Jo Mora at the unveiling of the Junipero Serra Memorial Cenotaph on October 12, 1924. Representatives from each of the twenty-one California Missions laid a bouquet of flowers at the base of the cenotaph. It was dedicated on October 16, 1924.

Pat Hathaway Collection

The young bear at Father Serra's feet symbolizes the young state of California, which Father Serra helped found. The history of the missions is depicted in carvings on the sides of the memorial. The fruits, grains and animals the padres introduced into California are represented in the carvings, as are those of the Portola-Crespi expedition in their quest of Monterey Bay, the Indians, the coat-of-arms of Castile and Lyon, Pope Pius VI and Charles III, the reigning pontiff and King of Spain at that time, the first baptism in San Diego and the fatal Indian attack there of Father Jayme.[52] Harry was there for the dedication of the Serra Memorial on October 16, 1924.[53]

Besides restoring Carmel mission, Harry acquired and replaced all the furnishings and artifacts that had passed into private hands while the mission was abandoned. On several occasions when he was a dinner guest at the rectory at San Carlos Church in Monterey, and while he was unobserved, Harry would remove vestments and take them to the mission. Harry believed adamantly that the articles belonged there, but when Father James Culleton, associate pastor at San Carlos Church, found the vestments at the mission, he told Harry he could keep them there, but he admonished him against taking any more. Nevertheless, all the valuables were returned to the mission at a later date.[54]

Harry was skilled at finding artifacts that were appropriate for Carmel and then repairing them. Kristina Foss, Museum Director at Mission Santa Barbara and an authority on the California Missions, said, "Carmel Mission would not be the beautiful mission it is if it had not been for Harry Downie.

Carmel had a fantastic, focused restoration program under Harry Downie. He cajoled, convinced, connived and in every way gained support for Carmel. There are things I could fault him for historically, but I can't knock the fact that the man was totally devoted to Carmel and managed to pull it together more than any other mission. It's just awesome what he did."[55]

CHAPTER 4

A NOTE IN A BOTTLE

No colonization without misrepresentation.

—Simeon Strunsky
American editor

Spain saw the establishment of the missions as a means of colonizing Alta, or upper California. Franciscan padres were to be responsible for civilizing the Indians, teaching them to work, converting them to Christianity and preparing them to become citizens of Spain. Soldiers were to be responsible for protecting the padres and the Indians. A mission was to be built at San Diego and one at Monterey. Both ports had been discovered previously. Future missions could radiate from the two sites. Monterey was to be the headquarters, and a presidio was to be built there, because Spain wanted to extend itself as far north as possible to check any Russian advance from the Aleutian Islands. Russian fur traders and explorers had been based in Alaska since the 1740s, and reports showed them encroaching upon the California coast. A presidio was also planned at Mission San Diego.[56]

So, in 1769, the first detachment of the Sacred Expedition, the name given to the first expedition to establish missions in Alta California, left Loreto in Baja California. Captain Rivera y Moncada and Father Juan Crespi and twenty-seven soldiers, driving a herd of horses, mules and cattle, left on March 24 and arrived in San Diego on May 14. The second detachment under the command of Gaspar de Portola, governor of Baja California, and Father Junipero Serra, less burdened with livestock, made the trip between May 15 and June 29. Three small ships, the San Jose, the San Carlos and the San Antonio, sailed from Cabo San Lucas and La Paz with supplies and equipment. The San Jose, carrying the food, was lost at sea. The first ship arrived in San Diego on April 11. Twenty-one sailors and several soldiers in the expedition died from scurvy, and most of the survivors were ill and unfit for work. Provisions were short and several Indians in the Rivera expedition died from starvation.[57] On July 16, 1769, Fr. Junipero Serra ordered a brushwood chapel erected on a hillside above the bay, and he celebrated Mass and dedicated Mission San Diego, the first of the twenty-one California Missions.[58] San Diego was the first European settlement in California.

The Indians did not like the soldiers at the presidio, and the mission was unsuitable for agriculture, so in 1774 it was moved to its present site, six miles inland in what is now called Mission Valley. In November 1775, hundreds of Indians surrounded the mission at night, looting and setting fires.

They killed Fr. Luis Jayme and a carpenter and a blacksmith. Fr. Jayme was California's first martyr.[59]

Two days before Fr. Serra founded Mission San Diego, Gasper de Portola and Fr. Juan Crespi and a party of sixty-two explorers left San Diego to look for Monterey Bay. They rode past it but they failed to recognize it, because when Sebastian Vizcaino explored Monterey Bay in 1602 he fabricated a description of a famous port, and he was determined to settle it.[60] The Portola-Crespi expedition found San Francisco Bay, but their food supply was depleted, so on November 11, Portola ordered the group to return to San Diego.[61] The San Jose was supposed to have delivered food and supplies to them, but the San Jose was lost at sea. On December 9, expedition members erected a large cross on the beach at Monterey and they left a message that read: "The land expedition is returning to San Diego for lack of provisions, today, December 9, 1769." The following day, they erected another large cross on a knoll above the beach hear the mouth of the Carmel River, for the San Jose or any other ship that might come. It bore a message: "Dig at the foot and you will find a letter." The letter, in a bottle, described their route, condition and decision. It also suggested the ship's crew that should find it might turn back to San Diego in the hope of sighting and relieving the land party.[62] With their provisions gone, the starving expedition began slaughtering their pack mules.[63] Near what is now San Luis Obispo, they saw grizzly bears. They killed one and feasted on it and they named the place La Cañada de Los Osos, The Canyon of the Bears. Today, it is simply Los Osos. A granite statue of a grizzly bear in the plaza of Mission San Luis Obispo commemorates the event. The expedition returned to San Diego on January 4, 1770.[64]

Meanwhile, the San Antonio returned to Baja California for provisions, but when the Portola-Crespi expedition returned to San Diego and Portola saw the wretched condition of the camp and learned the San Antonio had not arrived, he told Father Serra they would have to return to New Spain if relief did not come by St. Joseph's Day (March 19). That afternoon, a ship was sighted but it disappeared from view. Portola agreed to wait a few more days. Four days later, the San Antonio arrived. It was on its way to Monterey, but it lost an anchor and it doubled back to San Diego. Fr. Serra believed the sighting of the San Antonio on March 19 was an answer to a novena (nine consecutive days of prayers and devotions) to St. Joseph and ending on March 19. When Portola described the bay of Monterey to Fr. Serra, Fr. Serra believed Portola had been to Monterey Bay without realizing it. "You have been to Rome," he told him, "but you did not see the Pope."[65] On April 16, the San Antonio set sail for Monterey and Father Serra was aboard the ship. A land expedition with Portola in command left the following day. They arrived on May 24. The San Antonio, because of contrary winds, arrived on May 31. Portola, Fr. Crespi and a soldier returned to the cross on the beach in Monterey, and they realized it marked Monterey squarely. They found no evidence of a ship having been there, but they found feather-topped arrows and stakes sticking in the ground, signifying friendliness. A string of sardines dangled from one stake and a piece of meat from another stake. At the foot of the cross lay a heap of clams.[66]

CHAPTER 5

MISSION SAN CARLOS BORROMEO

*The bells they sound
on Bredon,
   And still the steeples
hum.
"Come all to church, good
people."
Oh, noisy bells, be dumb;
I hear you, I will come.*
        —Alfred Edward Housman
                English poet

Bells played an important part in the life of every California Mission. They pealed the hour of rising and the time of morning worship. They pealed the hour of work and the time for food and rest. They pealed welcome to guests and sorrow to families of the dead.

    Bells, hung for the occasion, pealed in Monterey Bay on Pentecost Sunday, June 3, 1770, when Father Junipero Serra founded Mission San Carlos Borromeo, and named it for Saint Charles Borromeo, Archbishop of Milan.[67] A cross was erected and Father Serra blessed it and celebrated Mass in a chapel of branches under an oak tree where Carmelite padres celebrated Mass in 1602 when Sebastian Vizcaino sailed into Monterey Bay. A table served as the altar. Gaspar de Portola, governor of Baja California, took formal possession of Alta California in the name of King Carlos III of Spain, as soldiers stood at attention and the Spanish flag was unfurled near the cross.[68]

The following day, construction began on the church and the presidio. The structures were temporary, upright poles driven into the ground, close together, and filled with brush and plastered with mud inside and out. The roofs were made of the same material and covered with a thick coating of soil. The floors were the ground.[69]

Father Serra requested permission to move the mission to its present site near Carmel because Monterey was unsuitable for growing crops or raising livestock. Also, he wanted to get the Indians away from the influence of the soldiers at the presidio.[70] After receiving permission to move, Father Serra directed some of the construction of the mission at the new site. As in Monterey, the buildings were made of poles, brush and mud, and they were temporary. On August 24, 1771, on the feast of St. Bartholomew, a large cross was erected in the center of the quadrangle. Father Serra blessed it and celebrated the first Mass in Mission San Carlos Borromeo in Carmel. On December 24, he moved into the new building surrounded by a stockade about 130 by 200 feet, including a guardhouse for six soldiers and their families.[71] The present church was the seventh one. The cornerstone was laid on July 9, 1793, on the site of the fifth church, nine years after Father Serra's death.[72] Father Fermin Lasuen was in charge of construction.

New Spain hired Esteban Ruiz, a master stonemason, to build the church. He used sandstone, and mortar made from abalone shells. Indians quarried blocks of stone and hauled them to the mission in carretas, two wheeled wooden carts bumping along behind yokes of oxen. Abalone shells were found in a deserted Indian village where the Highlands Inn is now.[73] Ruiz made the walls of the church five feet thick and he curved them near the top to form a catenary arch, common in cathedrals and in Gothic architecture, and noted for its ability to withstand weight. The Gateway Arch in St. Louis, Missouri is an example of a catenary arch. The tower is of Moorish design and holds nine bells. They were removed for safekeeping in 1834 when the mission was secularized and abandoned.[74] The church was dedicated in September 1797. It is 167 feet four inches long and thirty-nine feet wide except for the sanctuary and baptistery, which vary from fifty feet four inches to sixty-two feet.[75] A piece of the ancient oak tree where Carmelite padres celebrated Mass in 1602 and Father Serra dedicated the mission 168 years later is on display in the mission museum.

Helen Hunt Jackson believed Mission San Carlos Borromeo "was perhaps the most beautiful, though not the grandest of the mission churches; and its ruins have today a charm far exceeding all the others. The fine yellow tint of the stone, the grand and unique contour of the arches, the beautiful star shaped window in the front, the simple yet effective lines of carving on pilaster and pillar and doorway, the symmetrical Moorish tower and dome, the worn steps leading up to the belfry—all make a picture whose beauty, apart from hallowing associations, is enough to hold one spell-bound."[76]

The abandoned church in Monterey became the site of the Royal Presidio Chapel, La Capilla Real, built in 1794 to serve the soldiers of the presidio. A piece of the ancient oak is housed there also. Esteban Ruiz designed the façade. It is the only building remaining from the original presidio. Hippolyte de Bouchard destroyed the presidio buildings when he ransacked Monterey. Bouchard, a French-born privateer sailing under the flag of Buenos Aires, looted and burned Monterey from November 20 to 27, 1818.[77] The Royal Presidio Chapel is not one of the missions. It is California's first cathedral, and it was dedicated as a national landmark in 1961. Today it is a parish church, San Carlos Cathedral, the oldest continuously functional house of worship in California.[78]

Harry hewing the log for the cross he erected
on the Monterey Beach in 1969
Courtesy Monterey Diocese Archives
Ron James, Photographer

A monument to Fr. Junipero Serra, overlooking the site where he landed in Monterey on June 3, 1770. Jane Stanford, wife of Leland Stanford, commissioned the granite memorial, and it was dedicated in 1891.

Photo by Dolores Billman

CHAPTER 6

THE BIRTHPLACE OF CALIFORNIA

*Even his griefs are a
joy long after to one
that remembers all that
he wrought and endured.*

—Homer
Greek poet

One hundred seventy-five years after the Portola-Crespi expedition planted a cross on a knoll above Carmel beach in a vain plea for rescue, Harry hewed a redwood log into a cross and erected it in place of the original one to commemorate the event.[79] In November 1983, termites, old age and a fierce wind storm brought Harry's cross down. In January 1984 a, small group of citizens, fearing the state of California would not replace the cross, erected a new one on the same site without asking permission. They entered state property through an unlocked gate at Bay School and as they unloaded the cross from the back of a truck, they kept an eye out for peace officers.[80] "We did it with fear and trepidation," a woman in the group said.[81] The cross is accessible only by a footpath. A granite rock along the path bears an inscription which reads: "On December 10, 1769, the Portola-Crespi expedition from Mexico erected a cross on this hill to signal its long overdue supply ship, San Jose. A message at the cross stated that they were suffering great privation and were returning to San Diego. The San Jose had been lost at sea."

An inscription on a granite rock along the path leading to the cross on a knoll above Carmel beach.

Courtesy Robert Kirchner

The cross the Portola-Crespi expedition erected on the Monterey beach resulted in the founding of Monterey. On December 9, 1969, city, county and state officials along with the Old Monterey Bicentennial Committee assembled on the Monterey beach to celebrate the 200th anniversary of its placement. The celebration began with a marching band led by a color guard, all in Spanish costume, as were members of a choir. Members of pioneer Monterey Peninsula families, some of them descendants of members of the Portola trek, were on hand in costume. Harry had hewed a redwood log into a cross, and he erected it on the beach. A telegram was read from Lt. Gov. Ed Reinecke congratulating Monterey on the launching of its Bicentennial year, of which the raising of the cross was the first official function. Bishop Harry A. Clinch blessed the cross with holy water, using a silver vessel brought from Mexico by Father Junipero Serra. Harry told the participants in the ceremony that he made the cross from redwood because of its resistance to the elements, and Father Juan Crespi was the first non-native to see the tall trees with the reddish bark, near Pinto Lake, close to the present site of Watsonville. He named them Palos Colorados, redwoods.[82] A plaque at the base of the cross gave a brief history of the monument and noted that it was donated by the citizens of Monterey to mark the city's 200th birthday, but in September 2009 vandals sawed the cross off at the base. It was never replaced.[83]

On July 16, 1969, the United States Postal Service issued a six-cent postage stamp to commemorate the colonization of California beginning with the founding of Mission San Diego on the same day, 200 years earlier. The belfry of Carmel Mission Basilica appeared on the stamp.[84]

John Billman

Our Lady of Bethlehem, Patroness of the Diocese of Monterey, California's oldest statue.

Monterey Diocese Archives. Photo by Patricia Rowedder.

CHAPTER 7

OUR LADY OF BETHLEHEM

*Saints will aid if
men will call: For
the blue sky bends
over all.*

—Samuel Taylor Coleridge
English poet

When the Sacred Expedition was preparing to leave, the Archbishop of Mexico City presented an almost life-size statue of Nuestra Señora de Belen, Our Lady of Bethlehem, to Jose de Galvez, the Visitador-General of New Spain, Spain's colonial administrator who conceived the plan to colonize and develop Alta California as a source of revenue for Spain. Our Lady of Bethlehem was to be the Conquistadora, the Conqueress of California. The statue was taken to San Blas and enshrined on the vessel San Antonio. When it arrived in San Diego, the statue was taken in solemn procession to the altar where Father Serra celebrated Mass for the founding of the first mission in California on July 16, 1769. When the San

Antonio arrived in Monterey, the statue was taken in solemn procession again to the altar where Father Serra celebrated Mass for the founding of Mission San Carlos Borromeo on June 3, 1770. When the mission was moved to Carmel the statue was moved there and it was always in the various churches of the mission.[85]

Sailors, grateful for safe returns from voyages at sea, trekked over the hill from the port of Monterey to give thanks to Our Lady of Bethlehem. Devotion to her under the title Belen began when Portuguese explorer Vasco de Gama, the first to reach India in 1498, attributed his success to his devotion to her. King Emanuel I of Portugal changed the name of Restellon, near Lisbon, to Belem, and he built a church there in Our Lady's honor, Nossa Se hora de Belem. From that time, prayers to Our Lady of Belem were on the lips of Portuguese adventurers, from whom Spanish navigators acquired the devotion to her, Nuestra Se ora de Belen.[86]

About 1850, when the ceiling over the sanctuary in the church began to show signs of collapse, statues and other movable items were taken to Monterey for safekeeping. The statue of Our Lady of Bethlehem was put in the sacristy. From there, it was taken to people's homes where the faithful could offer their devotion to her.[87]

When Harry learned that a woman in Carmel had a statue of a saint in her house, he asked her to let him see it. The woman had taken the statue to Oakland when she moved there, and she brought it with her when she moved back to Carmel years later. The clothing had been burned, termites had eaten the wooden base and the arms were disjointed.

Harry persuaded the woman to let him restore the statue, and he took it to the mission and began working on it. During a discussion with the woman, he discovered the statue's identity. It was Our Lady of Bethlehem, the Conqueress of California, Patroness of the Diocese of Monterey, California's oldest statue. Harry told the woman she was not going to get the statue back. "It was too important," he said. "It belonged in the mission." The woman understood Harry's concern. At Midnight Mass on Christmas Eve, 1944, Our Lady of Bethlehem returned to her home in Carmel Mission after an absence of a century.[88] Christmas Eve was chosen as the appropriate time to restore her to the altar at the mission church because of the significance of her name. Father O'Connell re-blessed her before Mass. After Harry built the reredos (wooden backdrop behind the altar) in 1956, he enshrined Our Lady behind glass, in a prominent place in the Mortuary Chapel. He dressed her in a silver embroidered gown, made in Mexico and estimated to be 250 years old. He placed his mother's hair on her head, his grandmother's gold engagement ring on her index finger, and a gold necklace given to his mother when she was born—around the neck of the infant Jesus she is holding. Two small heart-shaped lockets adorn the necklace. One holds a photo of Harry's mother, and the other holds a photo of Harry's daughter, Miriam. Our Lady's gold acorn earrings were a votive offering by the woman who had her in her house. They were made by the first jeweler in Monterey. Her ears were pierced to receive the earrings, and they had been on her for many years.[89] The silver crown she is wearing is inscribed with the words, "From the devotion of

Naval Lieutenant Juan Bautista de Matute, Commander of the frigate Purisima Concepcion. He dedicates this crown in fulfillment of a vow, year 1798."[90]

Mission Indian Woman, Carmel, California, 1880

Path Hathaway Collection

CHAPTER 8

CAPTAIN OF THE INDIANS

Of all the wonders that I
  yet have heard;
It seems to me most
  strange that man should
  fear;
Seeing that death, a
  necessary end, will
    come when it will come.
      —Shakespeare *Julius Caesar*

The Mortuary Chapel is a side room of the main church. It was built in 1821 as a mortuary for the Indians. When they died, their bodies were wrapped in their blankets and placed in the Mortuary Chapel for two days before being buried in the cemetery. From 1771 to 1833, more than 2,300 Indians were buried in the cemetery. They were buried in rows, and as the bodies in the rows decomposed, more bodies were added to the rows. After the mission was abandoned, Indian families who had moved away continued to take their dead to the cemetery for burial.[91] The Mortuary Chapel was in constant use as an entry to the church. The front door of the church was rarely used. The stone doorway of the Mortuary Chapel is original and is composed of three architectural styles. The columns are Gothic, the arch is Moorish and the frieze is Greek. Originally, the large crucifix over the main altar in the church was in the Mortuary Chapel, which was known as the Chapel of the Passion, because the design on the ceiling represents a passionflower.[92]

Adobe walls twelve feet high once enclosed the cemetery, but gradually rains washed the walls away and raised the level of the cemetery, and water began seeping into the church. Harry found the original level of the cemetery in 1932 when he excavated down to the level of broken tiles from the old roof of the church.[93] He also unearthed the bowl from the mission's original baptismal font. He restored it and carved an oak cover for it and placed it in the baptistry inside the entrance to the church.[94] In renovating the cemetery, Harry built mounds of dirt at random to represent graves, placed crosses on them, and in keeping with Indian tradition, decorated the mounds with abalone shells. First, he dug a pit in the cemetery and re-buried the remains of hundreds of Indians. "They will have a hard time getting through each other's bones on Resurrection Day," he once quipped.[95]

In October 1964, Harry was named "El Capitan" of the Carmel Mission Fiesta, a title previously bestowed upon Indians. "I was the last Captain of the Indians," Harry said. The Rev. Edward Poschen, assistant pastor and coordinator of the event, presented Harry with a medal.[96] Harry loved the

Indians just as Father Serra loved them, but they could try the patience of a saint. Andrew Gomez, a descendant of Mission Indians, was in the habit of asking Harry, "Could I borrow fifty cents?" One day, Harry said to him, "Say Andrew, you're always borrowing this money. Why don't you return it once in awhile? You never pay it back." "Well," Andrew replied, "I'll pay it back." Andrew went to Harry's house to ask his wife Mabel, who he had known since she was a young girl, to lend him fifty cents. Then he returned to the mission and paid his debt to Harry, and he asked him, "Now can I borrow fifty cents?"[97]

CHAPTER 9

A YEAR OF EARTHQUAKES

*Mile-stones on the
road of time.*

—Sebastian Chamfort
French satirist

1812 was a year of earthquakes in California. It became known as "el año de Los Temblores," the year of the earthquakes.[98] Seven missions were damaged, some so severely they had to be abandoned and replaced by new structures. At Mission San Juan Capistrano on December 8, during Mass on the feast of the Immaculate Conception, the walls swayed back and forth dumping the massive concrete ceiling on the congregation. Forty Indian worshipers were crushed to death.[99] At Mission La Purisima Concepcion on December 21, the walls tumbled inward and the hillside behind the mission opened in a great crack, emitting water and black sand.[100] A new mission was built in a valley four miles inland. It was built in a linear layout, most likely because of the effects of the earthquake on the original mission. All the other California Missions except Mission San Rafael were built in the forms of quadrangles.

Some quadrangles gave way to modern encroachments, while others crumbled back into the soil. Harry restored the original quadrangle of Carmel Mission, using only his eyes for reference. "I learned archaeology by experience," he once admitted. He had documents and sketches of the old mission buildings for guidance, but he relied on careful excavation in his restoration. "When you excavate carefully you get the outline of the buildings. All the restored buildings are on the original foundations. The church and museums, which used to be the padres' quarters, rest exactly as they were." [101]

Harry attended school through the sixth grade. "I'm a self-educated animal," he once said,[102] but in the process of restoring the missions he learned architecture, archaeology, masonry, history and art and he acquired one of the oldest and best libraries in California. Writers and historians consulted him for his expertise. His research took him to Mexico City and to Mallorca, Junipero Serra's birthplace. The editors of Sunset Books, for whom Harry once served as a consultant, referred to him as "the one-and-only Harry Downie, veteran restorer of missions and a walking encyclopedia of mission fact and lore."[103]

Many of the 300,000 adobe bricks Harry used in the restoration were made from the washed-out bricks and soil excavated from the ruins.[104] The roof tiles were made in forms. "It was a myth that the Indians made tiles over their thighs," Harry said. "You wouldn't find an Indian big enough to make a tile over his thigh. Tiles were 22 inches long and longer, and to form the tile over the thigh and let it cure in the sun, you would have had Indians lying all over the place for days," he said.[105]

On December 14, 1939, Harry accidentally discovered the exact location of the cross that Father Serra erected in the mission courtyard on August 24, 1771. He was digging a hole to plant a pepper tree when he struck a circular stone with a hollow center, and he found the bottom of the cross, small dusty fragments of wood mixed with the soil. Today, they can be seen in the mission museum in a miniature replica of the cross. Harry identified the location by an old sketch of the cross and a description of it. He hewed a new ten-by-ten-inch cross rising nearly fifteen feet and he placed it on the exact spot of Father Serra's cross. The design of the cross with its peculiar cap piece was copied from the engraving made by artist John Sykes of the 1792 Vancouver expedition. The original stones that Father Serra put there are still supporting the present cross.[106] On July 14, 1940, the Most Rev. Robert Armstrong, bishop of Sacramento, blessed the new cross. An inscription on a tile at the base of the cross identifies it.[107]

Harry's old room in the padres' library was the first library brought to California, and it dates from 1770 when Father Serra brought the first books from Baja California. The library was housed at Carmel Mission from 1771. Numerous books were added after Father Serra's death. By 1850, when the mission was in disrepair, all the books were taken to Monterey for safekeeping and kept by the pastors in the various houses used as rectories. Valuables including building materials were subject to theft and vandalism as well as the vagaries of the weather. In 1949, when the restoration of the library was completed, the books that had been housed in Monterey since the 1850s were returned, and the library is now in its original place in the restored padres' quarters.[108]

When Ronald Reagan took the oath of office for his first term as California's governor on January 2, 1967, he used a bible believed to have belonged to Father Junipero Serra and brought by him from Loreto to San Diego in 1769, to Monterey in 1770 and to Carmel in 1771. The bible is on display in the Carmel Mission Museum. "It is to my knowledge the oldest bible in California," Harry once said.[109]

Molding the bricks

Courtesy Mission San Fernando

Removing the mold

Courtesy Mission San Fernando

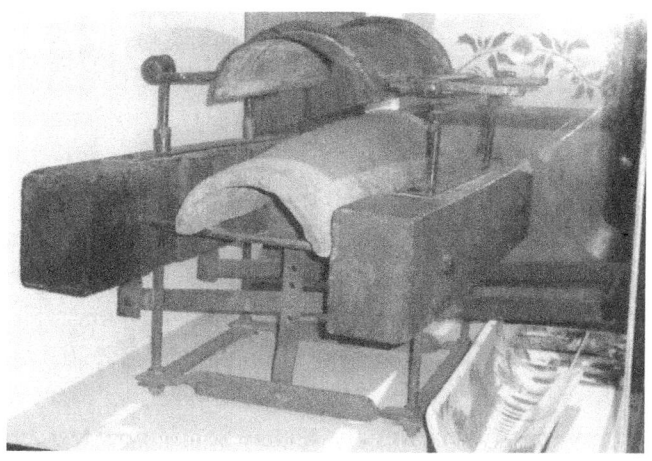

A tile making form used for making roof tiles at Mission San Fernando.

Courtesy San Fernando Mission

CHAPTER 10

THE FOUNDER OF CALIFORNIA

The history of the world is but the biography of great men.

—Thomas Carlyle
English essayist
and historian

Father Serra was born on November 24, 1713, in Petra, on the island of Mallorca, Spain. His baptismal name was Miguel Jose, but at sixteen he entered the Franciscan order and took the name Junipero, the name of a companion of Saint Francis of Assisi, founder of the Franciscan order. At five feet three inches tall, a special habit had to be made for him.[110] He was awarded the title of "Lector of Philosophy," and in 1740 he began his teaching career.[111] In 1749, he sailed to Vera Cruz to begin serving as a missionary in New Spain, now Mexico. He and Father Francisco Palou walked 270 miles to Mexico City. An insect bite left his leg ulcerated, and it plagued him for the rest of his life. He founded five missions in the wilderness, and he was named presidente of the missions with headquarters in Loreto, New Spain.[112] At fifty-six, Jose de Galvez chose him to join the Sacred Expedition to establish missions in Alta California. He rode 750 miles on muleback up the Baja peninsula to San Diego.[113] He founded missions and he baptized Indians. He was given the right to confirm them as well, a privilege afforded to bishops, but there were no bishops in the wilderness.

He was one of two men chosen to represent the state of California in the Capitol's Statuary Hall in Washington, D.C. He was chosen because he was a founder of California. When the statue was unveiled in 1931, Senator I. B. Dockweiler said in part: "This man whose memory is one with the epic of California was great in his humility. He triumphed by his courage when everything was bound to discourage him. He is worthy of first place among the heroes who created our nation, so his memory will never die and his name will be blessed from generation to generation."[114]

On October 16, 1963, President John Kennedy signed into law the creation of a national medal to commemorate the 250th anniversary of Fr. Serra's birth, which President Kennedy called a "reminder of our Spanish heritage, whose values were exemplified in the piety, courage and vision of Fr. Serra." The medals were struck at the U.S. Mint in Philadelphia, in quantities of gold, silver, platinum and bronze.[115]

On August 22, 1985, the United States Postal Service issued a forty-four-cent commemorative Junipero Serra airmail stamp. Father Serra's image appears on the stamp, and a mission belfry is in the background.[116]

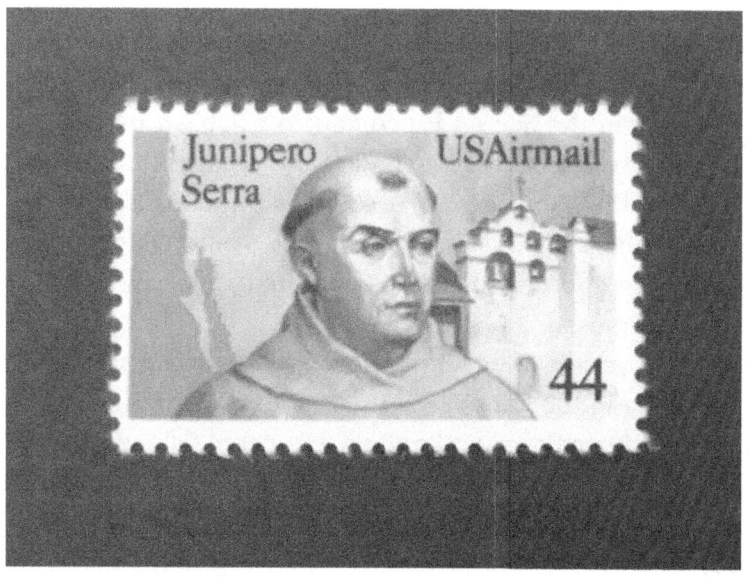

In 1769, Father Serra became the first father-president of the California Missions and he presided over them from Mission San Carlos Borromeo. Despite his ulcerated leg, he traveled to all the missions, and he walked from Carmel to Mexico City to intervene for the rights of the Indians.[117] On August 28, 1784, he died at the age of seventy. All night long as he lay dying, Indians crowded into his tiny cell, weeping for their beloved padre, El Viejo, until the door had to be closed so the body could be put in the coffin. As soon as it was placed there, between six lighted candles, the cell was opened and the Indians were there with bouquets of flowers of various colors, gathered from the fields to adorn the body of their venerable father. Bells at the mission and the presidio pealed the doble, the double peal signifying death. The entire community assembled. The San Carlos, anchored in Monterey Bay, fired a cannon throughout the day at half-hour intervals, followed by cannon fire from the presidio.[118] Father Serra was buried in the sanctuary of the fifth church.[119] When the present church, the seventh, was built, it automatically placed Father Serra's grave in the sanctuary. In 1937, Harry restored Father Serra's cell. The floor and part of the wall are original. Harry referred to Father Palou's book, *Life of Fray Junipero Serra*, for a description of the cell, in which Father Palou wrote of a rush stool and a bed consisting of some rough-hewn boards covered by a blanket serving more as a covering than as an aid to rest, for he never used even a sheepskin covering.

On August 29, 1937, on the 153rd anniversary of Father Serra's burial, his cell was dedicated. Father Michael O'Connell, the pastor at the mission, celebrated Mass. Father Augustine Hobrecht of Mission Santa Barbara, Vice-Postulator, or working advocate of the cause of sainthood for Father Serra, spoke on Father Serra's holy life and argued his sanctity. Members of the Onesimo family, the last Carmel Indians, placed a floral wreath on the bed. Excelentisima Maria Field, a descendant of Esteban Munras, a prominent Monterey settler, placed a wreath on Father Serra's grave. Lady Field received her title in 1931 from King Alfonso XIII for her work in preserving the Spanish influence in California. *Life* magazine published photographs of the dedication, and *Time* magazine devoted a story to it, calling Father Serra "a preacher of burning zeal."[120]

One of Harry's proudest achievements was supervising the opening of Father Junipero Serra's grave in August 1943 for the investigation into the cause of canonization, the process of declaring a deceased person a saint. Harry was an official member of the ecclesiastical commission, which authorized the opening of the grave and he conducted the Recognition of Remains. He was one of two laymen allowed to touch the bones of Father Serra. "I held Serra's remains in my own hands," Harry once said softly. Harry was a valuable witness at the canonical trial that investigated Father Serra's life. He helped prepare the report for the Secret Congregation of Rites and his testimony is included in the half-ton of documentation submitted to the Holy See.[121] The "Servant of God," as the candidate is known during the processes, may first be declared Venerable, then Blessed and finally saint. On May 9, 1985, Pope John Paul II declared Father Serra Venerable and on December 11, 1987, he declared him Blessed. He was beatified in recognition of his heroic virtues. Beatification is a declaration that he is blessed and worthy of Veneration, the last step before sainthood.[122] On September 23, 2015, Pope Francis canonized Father Serra and declared him a saint.

On August 28, 1984, on the Bicentennial of Father Serra's death, the U.S. Congress and the California Legislature declared the day as the "national day of recognition of Junipero Serra." All of California's bishops assembled at Carmel Mission Basilica for a commemorative Mass. Leon Panetta, then a U.S. Congressman, eulogized Father Serra in the House of Representatives.

Congressman Panetta said: "Junipero Serra is to the Pacific Coast what the Pilgrims are to New England, a founding father. . . . He represents the beginning of American history from their western perspective . . . and a striking contrast to the other explorers of our continent, driven not out of personal adventure or interest but from a spiritual mission. Father Serra sought not to conquer an unknown region but to cultivate its land and educate its people. . . . Let us now recognize his central role in the Spanish settlement of America and the national importance of his efforts."[123]

Harry Downie exhuming the remains of Father Junipero Serra in August 1943 for the investigation into the cause of canonization. Harry was a member of the committee that authorized the opening of the grave; he conducted the Recognition of Remains; he was a witness at the trial that investigated Father Serra's life, and he helped prepare the final report to the Holy See. He was one of two laymen allowed to touch the bones of Father Serra. The other was an anthropologist and archaeologist.

Courtesy Monterey Diocese Archives

CHAPTER 11

A Papal Visit

Christianity is not a theory or speculation, but a life; not a philosophy of life, but a life and a living process

—Coleridge
English poet

In the early 1940s, San Carlos Borromeo's parish was growing and it needed a new rectory. Harry excavated the site of the Spanish soldiers' barracks, a long adobe building at the former quadrangle, and he measured the rooms. He followed the original foundation so closely that he placed the pillars for the porch on the west side of the building exactly where he found the decayed bases of the old supports. When he finished the building, he carved the table and chairs for the dining room. On June 2, 1942, Bishop Philip Scher blessed the completed rectory.

Bishop Scher believed the mission needed a parochial school. Father O'Connell secured the services of the Sisters of Notre Dame de Namur to be the teachers. Classes opened on February 15, 1943, in temporary quarters at the Sisters' home near Carmel, with an enrollment of approximately fifty students. The first commencement exercise was held on June 4 in the mission church. In December 1944, Father O'Connell announced that the construction of Junipero Serra School would begin within the week. About 27,000 adobe bricks were refashioned from crumbled adobe bricks left over from the mission days. Harry had excavated the south side of the quadrangle carefully in the 1930s, and he made drawings of the partitions and tile floors of the former dormitories for unmarried Indians. He built four classrooms on the foundations of the former rooms, and he adhered to the mission architecture, a low adobe structure with a red tile roof and a covered porch that faces the courtyard.[124] Each room is designated by an animal painted over the doorway instead of numbers. Each animal nibbles at a bit of food. The rabbit who marks the primary room enjoys a bit of grass, the squirrel over the door on grades 3 and 4 has a nut, the deer over the doorway for grades 5 and 6 crops at leaves and a bear is devouring a fish over grades 7 and 8.[125] On September 10, 1945, Junipero Serra School opened with an enrollment of ninety-nine students. Classes were held temporarily in Crespi Hall and the old rectory until the four new classrooms were ready on September 24.[126]

In 1950, Bing Crosby contributed $5,000 from the proceeds of his Pro-Am Golf Tournament in Pebble Beach to finance a playground at Junipero Serra School.[127] The gift was the initial contribution to a campaign to fund the restoration of the quadrangle by closing the open west side. As additional funds were received, Harry built the three remaining classrooms on the west side, from 1953 to 1955. In 1952, he built a small adobe convent, also on the west side, for the sisters who taught at the school. He built it on the site of the kilns used during the mission period for making tiles and for burning lime-rock and abalone shells and converting them to mortar.[128] The Monterey Peninsula Herald reported: "The school rooms and all other restoration work have been done by Harry Downie, who has the entire history of Carmel Mission at his fingertips."[129]

In 1947, Harry built the Blessed Sacrament Chapel to provide a smaller, more intimate place for devotions than the mission church. It is eighty feet long and twenty-one feet wide and seats 102 people.[130] He built it on the site of the former blacksmith and carpenter shops constructed in 1774. The children of Ann Sutter contributed $10,000 toward the construction, in memory of their mother. Harry interred Mrs. Sutter's remains in the chapel near the sacristy. A headstone marks her grave. Part of the chapel wall on the parking lot is original. It is the oldest adobe in California and the second adobe built at the mission. The first building housed the three rooms of the padres' quarters, including Father Serra's cell. Harry left a portion of the chapel wall exposed to show the type of construction used then, layers of rock between the adobe to hold the plaster. Bishop Aloysius Joseph Willinger dedicated the chapel on June 11, 1947.[131]

Harry designed and built the reredos, the decorated wall structure behind the altar, in 1956. A woman named Mrs. Hart contributed the money to pay for it.[132] The original reredos collapsed in 1849. That year, Bayard Taylor, whom Horace Greely sent to California to report on the Gold Rush for the New York Tribune, visited the mission and described seeing "a huge mass of gilding and paint."[133] Harry used the motif from the reredos in Mission Dolores, but he had to redesign the top because Mission Dolores has a flat ceiling.[134] One of his best references was a copy of an inventory prepared by Father Jose Maria Real on October 10, 1834, the day Mission San Carlos Borromeo was secularized.[135] Harry and an assistant spent seven and a half months carving the reredos in seventeen sections, three stories high. They painted them green, rose and blue and outlined them in gold. Harry measured the left side of the wall, which is wider than the right side, but the reredos fit into place. After restoring the statues, Harry placed them according to Father Real's descriptions, with some deviation for the sake of balance, but he placed the statue of Saint Charles Borromeo, the patron saint of the mission, in its original position at the top.[136] Father Real's inventory also helped Harry reproduce the pulpit Father Casanova built in 1884 that is suspended on the right wall of the church.[137] Harry restored the door to the pulpit. It is the only original door at the mission.

Harry drawing the plans for the reredos, 1956
John Livingston, Photographer. Courtesy Robert Kirchner

Mission San Carlos Borromeo has been designated a state and a National Historic Landmark, and on April 27, 1961, Pope John XXIII elevated the church to a Minor Basilica because it contains the remains of Father Junipero Serra and it is one of California's best-known missions. The title of basilica is assigned to churches deemed to have achieved antiquity, dignity, historic importance or significance as centers of worship. As a Minor Basilica, Carmel Mission enjoys certain papally granted privileges. Missions Dolores, San Diego and San Juan Capistrano have also achieved basilica status because of their historic importance. The title of Major Basilica is reserved for the highest-ranking churches in the world, such as Saint Peter's Basilica. Only seven basilicas have major status, and they are all in Rome.

Harry wanted Father Serra to be declared a saint so the pope would celebrate mass at the mission.[138] Father Serra had not been declared a saint, but on September 17, 1987, Pope John Paul II celebrated Mass at Carmel Mission Basilica during his visit to the Western United States. He delivered a homily titled "Father Junipero Serra and Evangelization." He began by saying, "I come today as a pilgrim to this mission of San Carlos, which so powerfully evokes the heroic deeds of Fray Junipero Serra and which enshrines his mortal remains. This serene and beautiful place is truly the historical and spiritual heart of California. . . ." The Pope said Father Serra was the Apostle of California, and he had a permanent spiritual influence over the land and its people. He was convinced of the church's mission to evangelize the world, and the way in which he fulfilled that mission corresponds to the church's vision of what evangelization means. He brought the gospel to the Native Americans, but he also became their defender and champion. He walked from Carmel to Mexico City to intervene with the Viceroy on their behalf—a journey that twice brought him close to death. As a result, he drew up a "Bill of Rights" for the improvement of missionary activity in California, particularly the spiritual and physical well-being of its Native Americans. We too, the Holy Father said, are called to be evangelizers, to share actively in the mission of making disciples of all people. "Much to be envied are those who can give their lives for something greater than themselves in loving service to others. This, more than words or deeds alone, is what draws people to Christ." "Our strength is not our own," the Holy Father said, "It is God's power shining through our human weakness." It is the strength that inspired Father Serra's motto: "Siempre adelante. Nunca atras."[139] Always go forward. Never turn back.

An inscription at the foot of the altar in the Mortuary Chapel commemorates Pope John Paul II kneeling in prayer before the image of Our Lady of Bethlehem.

Pope John Paul II at Carmel Mission Basilica, September 17, 1987

Courtesy Robert Kirchner

CHAPTER 12

A Steak in the Freezer

*Human affairs inspire in
noble hearts only two
feelings—admiration or pity.*
—Anatole France
French novelist and poet

Sister Francisca, of the Order of Carmelites Discalced (Barefooted), remembers Harry as forthright, a remarkable gifted man, and one who was always willing to admit when he was wrong.

Before she entered the Carmelite Monastery, Sister Francisca worked as a writer for *Modern Screen* magazine in Los Angeles. In 1941, she attended a preview of a movie starring John Garfield and the Lane Sisters. The story line did not impress her, but the setting did. Cypress trees overlooked a white sandy beach. The movie was filmed in Carmel, California. Sister Francisca had never heard of Carmel, but she wanted to go there. She started saving gas coupons for the drive because World War II was being fought in Europe and gasoline was rationed. Near Carmel she drove past an imposing building, which she later learned was a Carmelite Monastery, and which she was destined to enter exactly ten years from that date.

During the war, Sister Francisca worked for the Red Cross, and then as a public relations officer at Letterman Hospital. After the war, she returned to Carmel to take some time off. After attending Mass at Carmel Mission, she took a tour of the mission and it changed her life. When she saw Father Serra's cell, she said she stood transfixed. It was primitive compared to her room at the La Playa Hotel, she said, but she was inspired to live like that.

In 1951, on the night before Sister Francisca entered the Carmelite Monastery, she stayed in a room behind Harry and Mabel Downie's house. Harry told her he would put a steak in the freezer for her because she would be out in a few months.

The Carmelites do not eat meat. Twenty-five years later during a Mass at the monastery in honor of Sister Francisca's silver jubilee, the celebrant saw Harry in the congregation and he said to him, "You can take the steak out of the freezer now, Harry."

On one occasion, the Carmelites ordered a statue from Italy, of Our Lady of Mount Carmel, for the monastery chapel. The statue was huge, and when it arrived Harry said it would never fit in the chapel. Sister Francisca's hopes were crushed. Much later, Harry said, "We'll give it a try." It was a perfect fit.

After Sister Francisca's mother died, Sister asked Harry to put a swatch of her mother's hair on a statue of Our Lady of Mount Carmel in the church at Carmel Mission. Harry said he could not do it because her mother's hair was red, and Our Lady of Mount Carmel did not have red hair. When Sister Francisca showed Harry a picture of Our Lady of Mount Carmel with red hair, Harry put her mother's hair on Our Lady's head.[140] Sister Francisca died at the Carmelite Monastery on May 29, 2015. She was a nun for sixty-four years.

Rui (Roy) Barcelos remembers Harry as an interesting man, and a man who knew how to do many things. Harry always led group tours of the mission, Rui said. Rui worked for Harry from 1973 to 1978, after emigrating from the island of Terceira in the Azores. Rui gardened, worked where needed and drove Harry to his out-of-town trips. "Every week I had to take him somewhere," Rui said. Rui is a friendly man with a quick smile, and he enjoys reminiscing about Harry. His eyes brightened as he recalled walking into the church at Mission Santa Clara with Harry. Harry pointed to two statues he carved on the altar, and he said they were wearing his mother's dresses. Rui said Harry had a large black dog named Gaspar. Harry named him Gaspar because he was born on June 3, the date Gaspar de Portola claimed California for King Carlos III of Spain. Harry and Gaspar were inseparable. Gaspar was about thirteen years old when he died, according to Rui. Rui buried Gaspar in the garden by the present Sir Harry Downie Museum and the cork tree, as Harry stood by. "Harry cried," Rui said.[141]

Edward (Ed) Soberanes remembers Harry as a nice and humorous man. Ed traces his ancestry to the Spanish soldiers who accompanied Gaspar de Portola and Junipero Serra to California, one of whom is buried in the mission church. Ed was a Carmelite Brother for fourteen years, from 1956 to 1970, and he was the organist at Carmel Mission for thirty-eight years. "Harry used to tease me when I was a kid practicing the organ in the church loft," Ed recalled, saying, "Hey what's all that noise up there?"[142] "Harry ruled the roost at the mission," Ed said.

Huu (H-You) Van Nguyen remembers Harry Downie as a good man, a strong man, and a man whose work had to be done to perfection. "Harry wanted everything perfect," Huu recalled. Huu is a warm, friendly man, and he delights in talking about Harry.

Huu escaped from Vietnam in a makeshift boat with twenty-two other refugees on January 25, 1977, when he was twenty-two years old. The boat's engine failed, and a blanket was used as a sail. An American ship rescued them and took them to Singapore, where they stayed for three months.

From there, Huu and some of the others went to Danbury, Connecticut. Huu stayed there for two years. A Lebanese priest in Danbury sponsored Huu, and in 1979 Huu drove from Danbury, Connecticut, to Seaside, California, where his wife's uncle lived. "Connecticut was too cold," Huu said, but he is happy in Seaside.

Huu went to work for Harry Downie on March 19, 1979, and he has worked at Carmel Mission since then. Harry died one year later. "Harry taught me to do many things," Huu said. Huu is a man of many talents, but his artwork is remarkable. He has restored and painted altars at Missions San Fernando, San Jose and San Juan Bautista as well as Carmel. He gilded the reredos in the church at Carmel Mission. An artist submitted a bid of $60,000 to Fr. John Griffin, then-pastor, but Huu did the job for little more than $1,000. He braided the crown of thorns on the crucifix on the reredos. He painted and decorated the chandeliers in the Carmel Mission Church. He built and painted the reliquary which holds pieces of St. Junipero Serra's coffin. He made the spindles for the entrance gate at Carmel Mission. In 2004, the Vatican named Huu a Knight of St. Gregory the Great for outstanding service to the church.

At Harry Downie's funeral at Carmel Mission on March 13, 1980, Huu rang the church bell slowly—seventy-six times—one for every year of Harry's life.[143]

Emmett O'Boyle is a retired lawyer, and he has been a docent at Carmel Mission since 2008. Emmett and his family were friends of the Downies. Emmett remembered Harry Downie as warm, friendly and outgoing, and he said Harry protected the mission from the misdirected zeal of the clergy. No one could tell a story like Harry, and if you asked Harry a question about a mission, it didn't matter which mission, you would get a detailed answer. "Harry liked to tease my kids," Emmett said, and he added, "Harry's wife Mabel was a wonderful person. She had the patience of ten saints."[144]

Pat Hathaway has owned California Views Photo Archives since 1970. He met Harry Downie then and he used to take mission photos to Harry in order to identify them. "Harry was a walking encyclopedia," Pat said. "He always knew exactly where the photos were taken." Pat said, "When the church at Carmel Mission was burglarized, it broke Harry's heart. He died soon afterward."[145]

Carmel Mission was burglarized in March 1980. Harry Downie died on March 10, that year. Richard Menn, Harry's former assistant who succeeded him as curator of the mission, said the burglary killed Downie.[146]

When Your work speaks
for itself, don't interrupt.

—Henry J. Kaiser
American industrialist

In 1935, Harry hired two brothers, Robert Morton, age ten, and Don Morton, age twelve, to work as laborers at Carmel Mission for $1 a day, an excellent wage during the Great Depression.

Robert and Don were altar boys, and one morning as they

were putting on their cassocks to serve Mass, Harry asked them if they wanted to go to work. They accepted his offer.[147]

Robert remembers Harry as a good boss; you just had to do what he said. You would never argue with him. "He was a character," Robert said. "He was just Harry, take it or leave it. He never complained about anything or anyone. He seemed to be able to do anything, but he did everything his way, and his way always worked." Robert saw Harry as a father figure because his father died when Robert was about one year old.[148]

Harry made the pews in the church, and Robert and Don assembled the parts. Don took the parts from Harry and drilled holes in the pews. Robert was the glue boy. He heated the glue gun and inserted the dowels.[149]

When Robert saw an adz, an ax-like tool for hewing logs, he didn't know what it was. Harry said you're going to hew the logs for the rafters in the ceiling of the gift shop. Harry showed Robert how to use the adz, while straddling a log, and he told him to spread his feet apart when using it or he could cut his toes off. Robert spent the next two to three weeks adzing the ceiling for the gift shop.[150]

Tours of the mission cost fifty cents. A person in the gift shop would ring a bell, and Robert and Don would put on Franciscan-style robes and guide the tourists.[151]

In 1938, Harry bought some new lumber to make the doors to the main entrance to the church. He instructed Robert and Don to dig a ditch to certain specifications. Then he told them to put the lumber in the ditch, and he threw something white inside, probably lime. He added water and dirt, and he told the boys to cover it up. When they dug up the lumber a couple of weeks later, Robert said it looked 100 years old.[152]

When Harry restored Father Serra's cell in 1937, he asked Robert to get him some tarpaper. Harry burned the tarpaper, and the smoke discolored the new walls and made them appear antiquated.[153]

When an equipment operator exposed some original floor tiles, Harry told Robert to gather the tiles and take them to a room adjacent to Father Serra's cell. Then he showed Robert how to lay tile, and he left. "Harry was a good teacher," Robert said, "and he was patient," but when he returned and he saw Robert on his hands and knees, and laying tile from the doorway inward, he kicked him in the rear end, and he said, "You have to have a system! I don't care what you're doing; you always have to have a system."[154]

Robert and Don worked for Harry six summers in a row.

"We had a lot of fun working for Harry," Robert said. Don became a plumber, and later, an estimator/planner at the Naval Postgraduate School in Monterey. He died in 1992. Robert and his wife Golda lived in the Bay area. Robert became a flooring contractor, and he worked on large government and public buildings in Northern California and the Central Coast. He always remembered Harry's admonition: "You always have to have a system."

CHAPTER 13

SECULARIZATION

*Let the farmer forevermore
be honored in his calling,
for they who labor in the
earth are the chosen
people of God.*

—Thomas Jefferson

Before the first mission was founded in San Diego in 1769, not a single head of livestock or grain of wheat existed in California. Yet for almost sixty-five years, the padres and Indians at the missions raised livestock, grew crops, made wine, tanned leather and worked as carpenters and blacksmiths; and the Indian women cooked, sewed, spun and weaved clothing. By the peak of the missions' development in 1832, they collectively owned over 308,000 head of livestock and produced more than 2,214,000 pounds of grains. Mission San Luis Rey alone, near Oceanside, owned over 27,500 head of cattle and 26,000 head of sheep.[155]

In 1815, Fr. Antonio Peyri founded San Antonio de Pala,

about twenty miles inland from Mission San Luis Rey, as an assistencia, or assistant mission, to serve the Pala band of Indians who worked in the grain fields there. San Antonio de Pala has been in active use by the Indian population since 1815, and it is the only surviving assistencia in the mission system. At its peak it served over 1000 Indians, more than some of the missions.[156]

The missions conducted a flourishing business with trading ships—trading hides, tallow, grain, wine and olive oil for manufactured goods. Yet despite the missions' prosperity, civil unrest in New Spain eventually caused the missions downfall. In 1810, a movement for independence resulted in a series of wars. Government authorities in Mexico City seized the assets of the Pious Fund, an endowment established in the 17th century to fund missions in Baja and Alta California. Mission San Carlos Borromeo lost $800 a year, the salaries of its two missionaries. The mission was self-supporting, but the presidio stopped receiving supplies and the soldiers stopped receiving their pay. They had to depend on the missions for their support. The situation remained in effect for almost a decade.[157] Spain, already weakened when Napoleon Bonaparte deposed King Ferdinand VII and placed his own brother Joseph on the throne in 1808, stopped contributing to the missions as well, because of the hostilities.

Meanwhile, in 1812, Russian colonists built Fort Ross on the northern California coast. They armed it with cannons, grew crops, raised animals and hunted sea otters for their pelts, but by 1839 they had hunted them almost to extinction, so Russia withdrew their colonists.[158] Today, the reconstructed fort on the Sonoma County coast is a State Historic Park.

With the signing of the Treaty of Cordoba on August 24, 1821, New Spain declared its independence from Spain and proclaimed itself the Mexican Empire.[159] Yet Mexico celebrates its Independence Day on September 16, the date when Father Miguel Hidalgo in 1810 delivered El Grito (the cry) in the village of Dolores, to rally the people to take up arms in a war for independence.[160] On August 17, 1833, the Mexican government enacted a law requiring secularization of the California Missions. Mission lands were taken from the church and placed under control of Mexican civil authorities. Secular or parish priests were to replace the missionary priests and were to manage the churches as conventional parish churches. The missions were to be converted to pueblos, or parishes, and the Indians were to be given titles to the mission lands. Administrators, however, awarded land grants to prominent families and to retired soldiers recruited from Mexico to populate the pueblos and ranchos, and they slaughtered mission cattle to sell the hides and tallow to enrich themselves. The Indians were unable to manage their own affairs and they drifted away from the mission lands like a fog bank in the sunshine. Of 15,000 Indians in the mission system at the time of secularization, scarcely 5,000 were left by 1840. The Franciscans' dream of assimilating the Indians into Spanish culture was undone. In addition, after sacrificing their lives for the missions and the Indians, the missionaries were left to the mercy of the administrators and they often had to pay for the food they ate, food that they helped produce.[161]

Richard Henry Dana, Jr. witnessed the deterioration of the missions. In his classic *Two Years Before the Mast,* Dana wrote: "Ever since the independence of Mexico, the missions had been going down, until at last, a law was passed (Secularization) stripping them of all their possessions.... The great possessions of the missions are given over to be preyed upon by the harpies of the civil power, who are sent there in the capacity of administradores, to settle up the concerns; and who usually end, in a few years, by making themselves fortunes, and leaving their stewardships worse than they found them.... But the administradores are strangers sent from Mexico, having no interest in the country.... and for the most part, men of desperate fortunes—broken-down politicians and solders—whose only object is to retrieve their condition in as short a time as possible.... and the venerable missions were going rapidly to decay."[162]

Once a mission was secularized, its status as a mission ceased. Most of the missions were abandoned. Buildings where padres once meditated were used as barns, schools, jails, courtrooms, wineries and blacksmith shops. A pig farm operated at Mission San Fernando, and hay was stored in Father Serra's chapel at Mission San Juan Capistrano, the only surviving structure where Father Serra celebrated Mass. A print shop was in business at Mission Dolores as well as a popular tavern, the Mansion House. Gradually, most of the missions fell prey to the weather. Roofs collapsed when timbers rotted out beneath the heavy tiles. Once the roofs were gone, the rains washed away the adobe walls and they crumbled back into the earth.[163]

CHAPTER 14

RESTORATIONS

*Money is like manure,
of very little use except
it be spread.*

—Francis Bacon
English philosopher
and essayist

In 1948, the Hearst Foundation granted $250,000 to the Archdiocese of San Francisco and $125,000 to the Diocese of Monterey-Fresno to rebuild the missions in their jurisdictions. Bishop Joseph McGucken, acting administrator for the Monterey-Fresno Diocese, called Harry to ask him how the money should be spent. Harry suggested Mission San Luis Obispo needed to be restored, as well as Mission San Antonio, as it was almost a complete ruin. The rest, Harry said, should be spent at Mission San Juan Bautista.[164] Bishop McGucken sent Harry to Mission San Luis Obispo with a promise of $50,000 in restoration funding for the mission, but with a stipulation that $50,000 that had been collected for building a convent be used until the promised funds were received. A fire in 1930 destroyed the old convent. The promised funds created tension between Harry and Msgr. Patrick Daly, the pastor, who had to pay the restoration bills out of his parish funds until the check from the diocese came. By that time, Harry had spent approximately $45,000. Years later, Harry laughed and said the minute he presented the check to Msgr. Daly they became close friends, but until then a stony wall of silence existed between the two strong-willed Irishmen.[165]

Mission San Luis Obispo is one of the few missions that were never abandoned after secularization, but little work had been done to it since the exterior was boarded up and the ceiling and floor covered with wood, and a New England-style wooden steeple added about seventy years earlier. The wooden coverings remained in place until March 1920 when a fire gutted the sacristy.[166] The sacristy had never been refurbished. Harry said the church was in terrible condition. Everything became decrepit. It meant the complete restoration of the church. During the process, he said, rats and mice were his constant companions, running here and there.[167]

The bells are originals and, according to Harry, three of the finest bells in California. "They are very well shaped and have a great tone," he added. A man named Vargas cast them in Lima, Peru, in 1818. They were recast in Lima in 1878. Gregorio Silveira was the bell ringer at the mission, as were his father and grandfather before him. Harry said when old Gregorio rang the bells, he made music.[168]

When Harry began removing the wooden floor, he

discovered the original floor was made of mezcla, a lime plaster. Beneath the mezcla, he found the graves of three early mission padres buried near the sanctuary and the graves of two children buried near the entrance to the church. Harry identified the padres from the burial register, and he marked the graves with their names. A marble plaque on the wall gives the name of one of the children. Harry made doors that looked as authentic and as antique as the doors they replaced. He made the windows using glass from the old Hotel Del Monte bathhouse in Monterey, which had been torn down.[169] The Navy took over the hotel and grounds in 1943, and after the war, bought the hotel and it became the Naval Postgraduate School.[170] Harry bought the glass from the Navy Department as war surplus. It was thick, he said, and it lent itself very well to the restoration process. During the mission period, thinly scraped cowhides were placed over wooden frames and inserted in window openings. They let light in and kept the elements out. Harry enlarged the church in keeping with the growing parish. He remodeled a forty-foot-long wing made of brick, to conform to the main structure, and he added forty feet more to the wing. In digging through layers of limestone plaster, Harry learned the mission was once painted red. Cinnabar Ore, from which mercury or quicksilver, is extracted, is found in the Santa Lucia Mountains between San Luis Obispo and Salinas. It was burned and ground into powder and added to the whitewash to make it red.[171]

Harry wanted to recreate the altar as it would have appeared during the mission days, so he threw out the white altar that was purchased from a church supply house after the 1920 fire. Then he built a wooden altar, but he could not simulate the green shades of verde antique marble and the texture on wood, of a type of marble not available in California. After numerous attempts, Gregorio Silveira, the bell ringer, said to him, "They painted the wood with turkey feathers, Mr. Downie." Harry found some turkey feathers at a farm near Santa Margarita, and they did the job.[172]

The clergy always lived in the old padres' quarters, and Harry knew from experience that could be a miserable place to live, so he built a rectory and he built a convent to replace the one that was razed by a fire in 1930.[173]

Mission San Antonio de Padua was abandoned for forty-eight years after it was secularized. Because of its remote location, thieves were able to steal roof tiles and anything else they could get their hands on. A shingled roof was built on the church but it decayed, and corrugated metal sheets were placed over the walls to keep the rain from washing them away. The church was filled with hay and manure from the horses that were kept in there at night. In cleaning the sanctuary, workers found outlines of the graves of padres. Harry opened the graves to verify the remains because looters dug holes throughout the mission while it was abandoned. The graves were found to be undisturbed. Msgr. John Sullivan, vicar-general of the diocese, and Harry's mentor at Mission Dolores, was present at the exhumation.[174]

The Hearst Foundation paid $50,000 for the restoration of the church, but the Franciscan Order paid for the restoration of the mission in its entirety because it was to house a school for the training of Franciscan lay brothers.[175] Harry and Brother Benedict O.F.M., an expert craftsman, worked with a crew of twelve to fourteen.[176] Harry stayed on to supervise the restoration of the quadrangle. The buildings had dissolved into heaps of dried mud. Only the church walls and twelve arches of the corridor remained.[177]

Harry began the restoration of the mission on July 14, 1948, 177 years from the day Father Junipero Serra founded the mission in 1771.[178] It was about a mile and a half southwest of its present location, but it was moved in 1773 because the water supply was better.[179] On May 16 that year, the first marriage in California took place in the mission church when Juan Maria Ruiz, twenty-five, of El Fuerte, Sonora, Mexico, wed Margarita de Cortona, twenty-two, a Salinan woman, of Mission San Antonio.[180]

In 1806, Father Buenaventura Sitjar O.F.M. built the first water powered gristmill and the first aqueduct in California, on the mission grounds. Much of the initial water system is still visible. In 1810, work began on the third and final church. It was 200 feet long and forty feet wide with adobe walls about six feet thick. The ceiling was built of large timbers that were floated down the San Antonio River. The church was completed in 1813. It is the same church that was reconstructed and is in use today.[181] The front corridor was restored as it was built originally. Bulldozers cleared mounds of dissolved adobe bricks until the original floor tiles and foundations were revealed. Then workmen swept the exposed tiles with brooms until the lines of the original buildings were clear. Brother Benedict and his Franciscan crew made almost 500,000 adobe bricks from the powdered remains of the six-foot thick adobe walls.[182] The rooms were reconstructed on the old foundations. The graves of American settlers were found on the north side of the church in a large mound of adobe used in the restoration. The bodies were reburied in the front porch of the church. Harry used pieces of broken tile that he found on the grounds to build the steps leading up to the church. No tile is on the church floor except on the steps to the altar. The original floor was covered with mezcla.[183] During construction, Harry transplanted a pomegranate tree from the patio to the north side of the church, around the corner from the front steps, where it continues to thrive.[184] The four statues on the altar are originals from the mission days: St. Michael and St. Anthony in a place of prominence, St. Francis of Assisi on one side, and St. Bonaventure on the other side.[185]

Harry had the use of a small house that had once been provided for a caretaker, but it had no furniture and no water, and no water was available at the mission. Harry had to bring his own water for a few weeks. Then the National Guard began providing water. The mission is on a military reservation. During the summer, Harry's family stayed with him and he and his family returned to Carmel on the weekends.[186] Harry's daughter Miriam was eight years old. She used to look forward each week to stopping in King City on the way home, for an ice cream cone.[187]

In its prime, 1,300 Indians lived at the mission, working at trades, growing crops and herding about 17,000 head of livestock.[188] Today, the restored mission tucked into the oak-studded Santa Lucia Mountains offers visitors a glimpse of life in the mission period.

Harry Downie

San Antonio de Padua Mission Foundation

417 MARKET STREET, ROOM 348 210 WEST SEVENTH STREET, ROOM 1008A
SAN FRANCISCO 5, CALIFORNIA LOS ANGELES 14, CALIFORNIA
YUKON 6-4159 TUCKER 8983

May 12, 1949

BOARD OF GOVERNORS
EDWARD ARNOLD
DON BELDING
E. W. BUCAHUR
CHARLES BROWN
ADOLFO CAMMILLO
GEORGE T. CAMERON
EDMOND E. COBLENTZ
RAYMOND V. DARBY
FRANK P. DOHERTY
ERNEST E. DUQUE
DOUGLAS FAIRBANKS, JR.
WILLIAM RANDOLPH HEARST
WILLARD W. KEITH
JOSEPH R. KNOWLAND
J. CLIFFORD LEE
GARRET MCENERNEY, II
JOHN P. MCINERY
DWIGHT MURPHY
GEORGE J. O'BRIEN
PAT O'BRIEN
JOHN O'MELVENY
GEORGE R. REILLY
JOSEPH SCOTT
PAUL A. SINSHEIMER
GRACE STURMER
J. F. SULLIVAN, JR.
JULIUS CHECONY
IRVING M. WALKER

PADRE ALFRED BOEDDEKER, O.F.M.
   Executive Director

CHESTER A. WETHINGTON
   Coordinator

HAL C. THOMAS
   Southern California Coordinator

Mr. Harry Downie
Carmel
California

My dear Harry:

Just a short note to let you know that the motion picture and television feature showing and telling about Carmel Mission as part of the story of "An American Heritage" turned out beautifully. I know you and the Fathers at Carmel will be very pleased. I'll try to let you know the first time it will be shown in Carmel or Monterey. It will be shown in Salinas at the Exchange Club, Monday, May 16th, at the "Big Hat" restaurant at twelve o'clock noon. Mr. Perry Henderson, Program Chairman of the Day and manager of the Telephone Company in Salinas, has asked us to invite you to be his guest at the luncheon, if you wish to attend.

I'm enclosing one of the thousands of clippings which are pouring in from every part of the United States. As you can see, Carmel Mission is mentioned.

Incidentally, I've heard you praised to the heavens for the wonderful job you are doing as architect of the San Antonio Mission restoration. Congratulations, Harry. Everyone I've talked to, and they number in the hundreds, have been most enthusiastic about your work.

I, personally, want to thank you for the kind help you so generously gave to me. I'm sorry I didn't get to see you after the radio broadcast from the Mission. I hadn't had any sleep for two nights and after working until four-thirty Sunday afternoon in that heat--I just folded up.

I'll be seeing you, Harry, and again thanks and keep up the good work.

Cordially,

Gordon Claycombe

A copy of a letter dated May 12, 1949, from the San Antonio de Padua Mission Foundation, addressed to Harry Downie, Carmel, California. Note the statement: "I've heard you praised to the heavens for the wonderful job you are doing as architect of the San Antonio Mission restoration. Congratulations, Harry. Everyone I've talked to, and they number in the hundreds, have been most enthusiastic about your work."

Courtesy Mission San Antonio de Padua Mission Foundation

The Board of Governors of the San Antonio de Padua Mission Foundation included William Randolph Hearst, publishing magnate; Don Belding, "Father of West Coast Advertising," who served Walt Disney and Howard Hughes, helped emerging Hollywood studios and built the Sunkist, Max Factor and Catalina swimsuit businesses; Joseph R. Knowland, United States Congressman, and editor, publisher and owner (at that time) of the Oakland Tribune; George R. Reilly, member of the State Board of Equalization for forty-four years, the longest tenure of any elected official in California history at that time; Grace Stoermer, banking executive and the first woman to serve as the Secretary of the California State Senate; John P. McEnery, a member of the Truman administration, and Chairman of the California Democratic Party. He was a supporter, confidant and floor leader for John F. Kennedy at the 1956 and 1960 Democratic Conventions; Eugene (Gene) W. Biscailuz, the 27th Sheriff of Los Angeles County. He was appointed Sheriff in 1932, and he was elected Sheriff from 1934 to 1958. He organized the California Highway Patrol in 1929, and he was a member of Los Angeles's first planning commission in 1920; Edward Arnold, Douglas Fairbanks, Jr. and Pat O'Brien were movie actors.[189]

Father Fermin Lasuen founded Mission San Juan Bautista on June 24, 1797, the feast day of Saint John the Baptist, or in Spanish, San Juan Bautista.[190] The church was seventeen feet wide and forty-two feet long. The mission was completed in 1798, but earthquakes destroyed it in 1800. From October 11 to 31 that year, as many as six earthquakes a day shook the area. Construction of the present church began in June 1803 and continued until June 1812.[191] The walls were made of adobe bricks and are three feet thick. The church is seventy-two feet wide and 188 feet long.[192] It is the largest of the mission churches, and the only one with three aisles, but in 1812 the padres filled in the open arched walls with adobe because they thought it would help support the heavy roof during an earthquake. When the restoration of the mission was completed in 1976 for the United States Bicentennial, all three aisles of the church were opened for the first time since 1812.[193]

In the 1860s, Father Rubio, the pastor, covered the ceiling and floor of the church with wooden siding and installed a New England-style steepled belfry. New England carpenters were in abundance in California after the Gold Rush. The steeple collapsed in a storm in 1915. The tower was remodeled in 1929, but Harry remodeled it and all the other woodwork in 1949. He said Father Rubio practically ruined the church.[194] About midway down the center aisle, oak leaves and coyote paw prints are imprinted on the tile floor, made when the tiles were still moist and drying in the sun.[195] The San Andreas Fault passes through the mission grounds. The 1906 earthquake knocked down one of the walls of the church.

Harry worked on the restoration of the mission from 1949 to 1950, and in 1976. "Harry was a genius," said Msgr. Amancio Rodriguez, former pastor of the mission. "There was no one else like him. He had an eye for building. We were fortunate to have restored the mission when we did." Occasionally someone would suggest doing something a different way, but Harry would clench his cigar in his teeth, glare for a moment and then say, "No we'll do it this way."[196] Harry taught the workers how to make the adobe bricks. They made them at the base of the mission cemetery, on a portion of the old El Camino Real, The Kings Highway. Originally, it was a foot trail connecting all the missions from San Diego to Sonoma. Eventually, El Camino Real became the main automobile road linking northern and southern California. Today, Highway 101 follows the original path of the padres, with a few deviations. It is often marked by standards bearing a facsimile of a mission bell, recalling the original reason for establishing the road.[197]

Mission San Juan Bautista faces the plaza of San Juan Bautista State Historic Park, an area of buildings that dates to the California of 150 years ago. The mission is not a part of the park, but visiting it is a quiet reminder of days gone by, when, as Helen Hunt Jackson wrote in 1883, "At San Juan there lingers more of the atmosphere of the olden time than is to be found in any other place in California."[198]

Harry built complete models of the missions to scale, and he spent months studying old drawings, photographs and church records before beginning actual restorations. Besides restoring Missions San Carlos Borromeo, San Luis Obispo, San Juan Bautista and San Antonio, Harry restored the interior of Mission San Buenaventura, and he rebuilt a portion of Mission Soledad. The Native Daughters of the Golden West funded the restoration, but it proceeded slowly as donations trickled in. Harry said it was difficult to work at Soledad because the wind blew sand into the adobe bricks as they were being made, and it created a hazard for workers on the roof. Harry was working on the roof one day when the wind blew his hat away and he was unable to find it. After that, the roof tiles were installed in the mornings before the wind started blowing.[199] The state of California restored Mission Solano in Sonoma, but Harry was appalled when he saw the lumpy walls, plastic statues and modern pews. After the State agreed to plaster over their work, Harry donated the interior furnishings including the stations of the cross and two statues he carved of Saint John and the Blessed Virgin.[200] Harry worked on the restoration of the Royal Presidio Chapel in Monterey in 1942, and in 1970 when the Bishop made it the cathedral of the diocese. He restored portions of the Plaza Church in Los Angeles, Colton Hall in Monterey, the Hearst Castle and historic buildings on the Monterey Peninsula and in San Juan Bautista. In addition, he served as a consultant during the restorations of Missions Santa Cruz, Santa Ines, Santa Clara, San Juan Capistrano, San Fernando, La Purisima and Santa Barbara.[201] He was often away from home for weeks at a time, returning home on the weekends.[202]

When Msgr. Francis J. Weber was teaching at the seminary at San Fernando Mission, he asked Harry to sketch the boundaries of the mission. Urbanization had cut into the 295 by 315 feet quadrangle and made it difficult to grasp the extent of the original layout without referring to a plot plan. Harry arrived one morning and then disappeared until dinner time, with his sketches. He had hired a pilot and he spent the day flying above the mission. "Even subterranean walls," he said, "are visible from the sky." Later, when Harry and Msgr. Weber went probing, Msgr. Weber said Harry was right on target.[203]

Harry had his feet in two centuries, the 18th and the 20th. He was as knowledgeable of the missions as if he had built them, and he was as familiar with the padres and explorers as if he had known them. He knew the plaster covering the walls of the church at Carmel Mission was made of abalone shells and he knew Fr. Serra used snuff. In restoring the California Missions, Harry recreated the mission period of California history and he preserved it for future generations.

Harry's closest friend was Fr. Maynard J. Geiger, archivist at Mission Santa Barbara, and a noted Franciscan historian, whose published works included *the Life and Times of Fray. Junipero Serra,* and a translation of *Fr. Palou's Life of Serra.* About once a year, Msgr. Weber would drive Fr. Geiger to Carmel, and they would stay in a room behind Harry and Mabel's house. Harry and Fr. Geiger quarreled continuously while remaining the best of friends. "It was a wonderful spectacle," Msgr. Weber said. Mabel had become blind, but she would cook their meals and then retire to the living room.[204]

CHAPTER 15

AN AMERICAN DA VINCI

*I believe the true
road to pre-eminent
success in any line
is to make yourself
master of that line.*

—Andrew Carnegie
Scottish-born American
industrialist

Harry Downie was knighted three times. In 1948, General Francisco Franco of Spain named him the Royal Knight Commander of Isabella La Catolica for his restorations of the California Missions, established originally by Spain. In 1954, Pope Pius XII made him a Knight of St. Gregory for a lifetime of outstanding work on behalf of the church, and in 1976 King Juan Carlos of Spain named Harry a Knight of Castle Belvere for his work in making the Spanish influence known. In 1949, the Academy of Franciscan History honored Harry for his "significant contribution" to the study of American Franciscan History, and in 1954 he was made a "Distinguished Member of the Association of the Friends of Fray Junipero Serra de Petra, Isla de Mallorca." In 1966, Mayor John Shelley gave Harry the key to the city of San Francisco for his part in California history. The key was modeled after a key Harry dug up at Mission Dolores when he was a boy. In 1967, the California Historical Society presented Harry with an award of merit for his work over thirty-six years restoring missions at Carmel, San Luis Obispo, San Antonio, San Juan Bautista, Soledad and Ventura. On January 23, 1969, the Monterey Peninsula Chamber of Commerce named Harry the Outstanding Citizen of 1968 and presented him with a commemorative plaque on which is inscribed: "In tribute to the man responsible for the restoration of Carmel Mission as erected by Fray Junipero Serra."[205] On April 22, 1971, Harry received the Elbert M. Conover Memorial Award for Religious Architecture.[206] Ted Durein, former managing editor of the *Monterey Peninsula Herald*, described Harry as "an American da Vinci with a Scots burr. He has the genius to do whatever work has to be done—regardless of difficulty. Whether he is restoring an old painting or raising the roof-tree of his new home all by himself or cooking the kind of enchiladas Padre Serra liked, Harry does everything artistically—but in his matter-of-fact way. He is that rarest of human beings—a Medieval Man."[207]

On January 12, 1955, Harry and Msgr. Michael O'Connell were the guests of honor at a commemorative banquet at the Naval Postgraduate School in Monterey. Seven hundred and fifty people attended. Harry was honored for his restoration of Carmel Mission, and Msgr. O'Connell was honored for his spiritual guidance during the restoration, as the first pastor at the mission since it was designated a parish.[208] Msgr. O'Connell gave Harry a free hand to do whatever he wished in his restoration work.[209] Harry and Msgr. O'Connell received commemorative scrolls. Harry's read:

> To Harry Downie, the well-beloved, cordial greetings. The community of Monterey Peninsula delights in phrasing its gratitude for the imaginative understanding and able services you have given in the restoration of the Mission San Carlos Borromeo. Founded by Father Junipero Serra and his colleagues the mission long neglected has again come to life and persuasive power because of your vision and your labors. It stands again in this troubled world a house of light shining with the love of Christ among souls along the uncertain paths of life.[210]

The Monterey Peninsula Herald published the names of all 750 guests.[211]

In spite of his reputation and his numerous awards, Harry remained a humble man. He was uncomfortable with the title Sir, bestowed upon him with knighthood. His favorite title was curator of Carmel Mission. Harry liked to sit in the courtyard with his dog Gaspar and observe the visitors. He would tell children he was Father Serra's brother and Gaspar was descended from Father Serra's dog.[212]

On one occasion, a woman was painting a picture of the mission, but she was pestering a work crew with so many questions about the mission that they could not complete their work. One of the workers complained to Harry, and Harry told the woman that she was "out of her province." "You have no regard for an artist," the woman hissed. "You had better stick to your pick and shovel." "You had better stick to your paint pot," Harry replied. The woman packed her paints and left in a huff.[213]

When Bishop Aloysius J. Willinger visited Carmel Mission, he stayed at the rectory and he slept in a twin bed that was narrower than the bed he was accustomed to sleeping in. The next morning at breakfast, the Bishop told Harry he fell out of bed during the night. Harry laughed. The Bishop said, "I'd fire you if I could get away with it."[214]

In 1978, after a student at Fresno Pacific University heard Harry interviewed at Carmel Mission Basilica, she was asked on a history test question to describe Mr. Downie in her own words as you would describe him to your students. She wrote:

> This man has done much for the restorations of the missions. He could be called "Mr. Mission." He had a great sense of humor, great knowledge and would be considered a scholar. Although he had received many honors, he downplayed these because he was also a very humble man. When you listen to him speak

about Serra or the missions, he seems to have lived in that time and is reporting as an eye witness. He had tremendous dedication and worked unceasingly for the restorations, and to correct history. His sleuthing ability paralleled Sherlock Holmes.[215]

August 25, 1972, was "Harry Downie Day" at Carmel Mission Basilica. Bishop Harry A. Clinch was the principal celebrant of a concelebrated Mass. Later, a crowd jammed Crespi Hall for dinner and a celebration of Harry's 69th birthday. The occasion also recognized Harry's cataloging of every book and artifact in the mission's collection, as well as his own large collection of books, paintings and artifacts. In addition, he served as the mission bell ringer until 1972, after which he played only on special occasions. "No one has to say the words," said Father George McMenamin of the mission. "The turnout is the testimonial. Harry Downie has a soft heart and a hard head. We've encountered both and we love him for it." Tears welled in Harry's eyes when Emilio Odello read the inscription on a bronze commemorative plaque honoring his forty-one years of work restoring Carmel Mission. "Presented to Sir Harry Downie K.S.G. by the Carmel Mission parish for his years of dedicated work in the sympathetic and authentic restoration of the Carmel Mission Basilica and its compound since 1931. Presented 1972." Today, the plaque is mounted on the wall of the entrance to the church.[216]

Harry had help with the cataloging. During the summer of 1971, Brian Shanley, a young economics teacher from New Jersey, helped Harry catalog all 579 volumes in the mission's library, the first library in California—and then Harry built the bookcases. Shanley spent three summer vacations working on the project. He described Harry as a rare genius. "You could almost call him 'second founder' of the mission. He not only has the mental ability to go back and do the research, but the engineering know how to have directed the reconstruction of the buildings on the exact site of their former founders."[217]

On February 28, 2012, an $18.95 Express Mail stamp was unveiled at a First Day of Issue ceremony at Carmel Mission. The image on the stamp depicts the façade of Carmel Mission against a backdrop of clouds.

Ruben Mendoza, a professor of archaeology at CSU Monterey Bay lent his expertise to the design of the stamp.

The gesture by the Postal Service "is indicative of the importance they attribute to the mission among the earliest settlements on this continent," said Knox Mellon, former executive director of the Carmel based California Missions Foundation.[218]

Carmel Mission
Often described as one of the most beautiful mission churches in the state of California, Carmel Mission is known for its dome-shaped bell tower and elaborate star-shaped window. Formally known as Mission San Carlos Borroméo del Río Carmelo, Carmel Mission was founded on June 3, 1770. It was the second in what would become a chain of 21 Spanish missions along the coast of California, each positioned about one day's ride on horseback from the next.

Interior ruins of Carmel Mission Church before 1884, facing front door

Courtesy Carmel Mission Foundation

Front of Carmel Mission Church before 1884

Courtesy Carmel Mission Foundation

Carmel Mission before restoration, date unknown

Courtesy Carmel Mission Foundation

Carmel Mission Church before restoration, c. 1910

Henry Meade Williams Local History Department,

Harrison Memorial Library, Carmel, California

Carmel Mission, c. 1882

Henry Meade Williams Local History Department,
Harrison Memorial Library, Carmel, California

Harry at Carmel Mission before 1936
Courtesy Monterey Diocese Archives

Harry with Father Michael O'Connell at Carmel Mission Construction site, 1940
Courtesy Monterey Diocese Archives

Harry with Father Michael O'Connell, 1940
Courtesy Monterey Diocese Archives

Harry and Mabel and daughter Miriam, 1941

Courtesy Monterey Diocese Archives

El Descanso, Harry and Mabel's house in Carmel. Harry built it in 1939 and he also made the furniture.

Courtesy Monterey Diocese Archives

Harry the chef

Courtesy Monterey Diocese Archives

Harry in front of the cross he erected on the site of Father Serra's cross, 1947

Courtesy Monterey Diocese Archives

Harry inside the Blessed Sacrament Chapel, 1950

Courtesy Monterey Diocese Archives

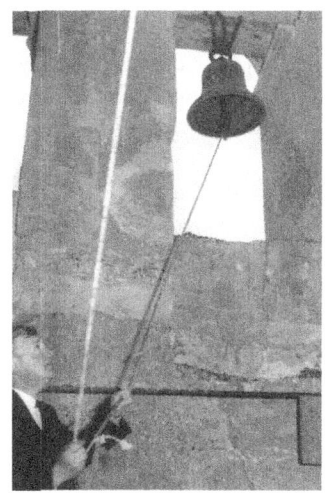

Harry ringing the bells in 1951 during the 167th Anniversary Mass of Father Serra's death. Harry was the bell ringer at the mission. "People tell me they know the mood I'm in by the way I ring the bells," he said.

Courtesy Monterey Diocese Archives

Harry playing bullfighter with Eddie Mestres. Eddie was the nephew of Father Ramon Mestres, pastor of San Carlos Church in Monterey, from 1893 until his death in 1930.

George Cain, Photographer. Courtesy Monterey Diocese Archives

Sir Harry, Knight of St. Gregory, 1956

Courtesy Monterey Diocese Archives

Msgr. Michael O'Connell and President and Mrs. Dwight D. Eisenhower at Carmel Mission on August 26, 1956. *Photo by Lee Blaisdell.*

Courtesy Monterey Diocese Archives

Harry with finished cross he hewed and erected on Monterey Beach in 1969

Courtesy Monterey Diocese Archives

Road to Mission San Carlos Borromeo and adjacent ruins, 1898.

J. K. Oliver, Photographer

Courtesy California History Room & Archives, Monterey Public Library

Harry Downie and John Yementes,
laying adobe bricks, about 1940

Courtesy Monterey Diocese Archives

Excavated ruins of padres' quarters in 1906

Courtesy Carmel Mission Foundation

Harry working on the south wing of Junipero Serra School at Carmel Mission, 1945

Courtesy Monterey Diocese Archives

Sir Harry Downie, Knight of St. Gregory, and Monsignor Michael O'Connell on January 12, 1955, when they were honored at a Commemorative Dinner at the Naval Postgraduate School in Monterey, for the restoration of Mission San Carlos Borromeo. Seven hundred and fifty people attended.

Photos provided by the author.

The reredos when Harry Downie completed them in 1956.

Arthur McEwen, Photographer.

Courtesy California History Room & Archives, Monterey Public Library

Harry Downie pointing out an area of concern on a model of Carmel Mission, to the pastor, Monsignor Michael O'Connell, 1969.

Paul R. Burgess, Photographer.

Courtesy California History Room & Archives, Monterey Public Library

CHAPTER 16

A Remarkable Man

*Si monumentum
requiris circumspire.
If you would see the
man's monument, look
around.*

—Inscription in
St. Paul's Cathedral,
London. Written
by Sir Christopher
Wren's son.

When Harry Downie was named the Outstanding Citizen of the Monterey Peninsula in 1968, Nick Lombardo, master of ceremonies, described him as having the tenacity of the Scots, from which stock he springs, and he said when he passes on there will be no need to lay a headstone because the historical monuments for which he has been responsible on portions of the Peninsula are epitomized in one great contribution to this beautiful part of California, namely the complete restoration of Mission San Carlos Borromeo.[219] Harry died on March 10, 1980, at his home in Carmel, and he was buried at the Carmel Mission cemetery beside the church he loved and restored. The only inscription on his grave is "Harry Downie, native of San Francisco." Cardinal Timothy Manning, Archbishop of Los Angeles, issued a statement upon Harry's passing, saying, "The church in California has lost a champion in the exodus of Harry Downie. He was custodian, chronicler and lover of our missions and the heritage they represented. Since everything on our earthly pilgrimage is only prophetic of our future home, may his love of God's earthly dwelling places be fulfilled in the heavenly abode."[220] Harry went to the mission six hours a day up to the time of his death, and he was serving as a consultant on the upcoming restoration of Mission San Jose in Fremont.[221] He was to have received an award on March 16, 1980, from the California Historical Society, for Historic Preservation.[222] His beloved wife Mabel died on April 24, 1981, and is buried alongside him. Miriam was the last survivor, and when she died there were no remaining Downies. Miriam knew she was terminally ill. When a carpet cleaner called her to schedule an appointment, she said, "I won't be needing your services. I will be moving to a new location."

When Congressman Leon Panetta addressed the House of Representatives in the nation's capital on July 1, 1980, on the subject, "Harry Downie: Bringing History to Life," he said, "Mr. Speaker, it is with great pride that I bring to the attention of my colleagues, the accomplishments of a friend and a remarkable man who resided in my district and who died recently." Congressman Panetta talked about the missions, and he said

John Billman

they exist today largely because of Harry Downie, who, for almost fifty years, dedicated his energy to the restoration of the missions and other historic sites around California. "Because of Harry's dedication," he said, "we have a living connection to our past." Congressman Panetta recounted Harry's numerous awards and he said, "Not only his fellow citizens but also kings and popes recognized Harry's accomplishments." He said he came to know Harry when he was a young boy attending Junipero Serra School at Carmel Mission. His presence was everywhere, working in the garden, repairing a door, designing an addition, researching history or helping the children or nuns. On Sundays, he was usually at the rear of the church making sure all was well. Congressman Panetta concluded his remarks by saying, "I am proud to have known Harry Downie, and I know that the communities in which he worked and lived are grateful to him for his life's work. He is no longer with us but the history he brought to life for us will always keep him alive in our memories."[223]

On August 25, 1980, Harry's birthday, the Sir Harry Downie Museum was dedicated following a memorial Mass in the basilica. The statue of Our Lady of Bethlehem, which Harry revered, recovered and restored, was placed on the main altar for the Mass. His Royal Majesty, King Juan Carlos of Spain sent a telegram of support, and sent an emissary for the dedication of the museum. Congressman Panetta spoke on "comments delivered on the floor of the House on the passing of Harry Downie." After Mass, the congregation followed the clerical procession along a pathway lighted by luminarias (candles inside sand-filled paper bags) to the steps of the museum where Barney Laiolo, Mayor of Carmel, unveiled a memorial plaque, which reads: "This building is dedicated to Sir Harry Downie for his devoted service to the restoration of the California Missions. August 25, 1980." Inside, visitors viewed photographs, artifacts, awards and citations received by Harry and a replica of his workshop on the mission grounds. [224]

Friedrich Wilhelm Nietzsche, the German philosopher, wrote, "Our destiny exercises its influence over us even when, as yet, we have not learned its nature: It is our future that lays down the law of today."[225] It was Harry's destiny to restore the California Missions and to preserve them for future generations. Harry became a cabinetmaker when he had other aspirations. He arrived at Mission San Carlos Borromeo on the 147th anniversary of Father Junipero Serra's death. He discovered the exact site of the cross that Father Serra planted in the mission courtyard on August 24, 1771, even though he was not looking for it, and he was still at Carmel Mission forty-nine years after stopping by for a brief stay.

Harry taking a break.
Patricia Rowedder, Photographer
Courtesy Monterey Diocese Archives

Harry and Gaspar taking a break.
Courtesy Monterey Diocese Archives

Carmel Mission Basilica
Courtesy Monterey Diocese Archives

Father Lawrence Farrell, Harry's boyhood friend who persuaded him to stop at Mission San Carlos Borromeo in 1931, delivered the eulogy at Harry's funeral on March 13, 1980, at Carmel Mission Basilica. Father Farrell said in part: "Do you feel as I do that Padre Serra had a hand in bringing Harry to Carmel forty-nine years ago? Harry was a blessing to this mission. Every mission and every historic building in California benefited directly or indirectly by his knowledge and practical expertise. Carmel was the recipient of his greatest attention and greatest affection."

"Harry had a sense of humor which was as individualistic as it was unique, and nowhere was it shown to better advantage than his dealing with the clergy and the hierarchy. By clever manipulations he protected the missions from misdirected zeal and he did this with such wit and originality that he left his one-time adversaries smiling. We shall miss you Harry, but we will never forget you.[226]"

End

EPILOGUE

THE MISSIONS IN THE ORDER OF THEIR FOUNDING

1. San Diego de Alcala. Founded by Fr. Junipero Serra on July 16, 1769, on a hill overlooking San Diego Bay, and named in honor of Saint Dedacus, of Alcala, Spain. It was the first permanent settlement in California. In 1774, the mission was moved six miles inland. In November 1775, hundreds of Indians surrounded the mission at night, looting and setting fire to the buildings. Fr. Luis Jayme and a carpenter and a blacksmith were killed. In 1780, the mission was rebuilt, but in 1803 it was destroyed by an earthquake. In 1813, it was restored and enlarged but it fell into disrepair. In 1931, it was restored in the image of the 1813 church. In 1976, Pope Paul VI designated it a minor basilica. It is in Mission Valley, five miles east of Interstate 5, off Interstate 8.

2. San Carlos Borromeo de Carmelo. Founded by Fr. Junipero Serra on June 3, 1770, in Monterey, and named for Saint Charles Borromeo, an Italian cardinal of the 16th century. In 1771, the mission was moved to its present site near

Carmel. It was the headquarters of the mission system, and Fr. Serra was the first father-president. He is buried in the present church at the foot of the altar. The church is the seventh one in a series that began with a crude shelter of logs. It was begun in 1793 under the direction of Fr. Fermin Lasuen, nine years after Fr. Serra's death, and it was dedicated in 1797. It is one of four mission churches built of stone. The others are Santa Barbara, San Juan Capistrano and San Buenaventura. Mission San Gabriel was built of stone and concrete up to the windows. On April 27, 1961, Pope John XXIII elevated the church to a minor basilica. It is at 3080 Rio Road, Carmel.

3. San Antonio de Padua. Founded by Fr. Junipero Serra on July 14, 1771, and named for Saint Anthony of Padua. In 1773, it was moved to its present site about a mile and a half farther north where the water supply was better. On May 16 that year, the first marriage in California took place in the mission church. In 1806, the first water powered gristmill and the first aqueduct in California were built on the mission grounds. In 1810, work began on the third and final church. It was completed in 1813. Some of the roof tiles were sold to the Southern Pacific Railroad and used on the roof of the Burlingame Railroad Station. It opened for service on October 10, 1894, and it was the first public building designed in mission-style architecture. In the mission's prime, 1,300 Indians lived there and worked at trades, grew crops and raised about 17,000 head of livestock. Today, the restored mission in the oak-studded Santa Lucia Mountains offers visitors a glimpse of life during the mission period. It is off U.S. Highway 101, twenty-three miles southwest of King City.

4. San Gabriel Arcangel. Founded by Frs. Pedro Gambon and Angel Somera on September 8, 1771, and named for the arcangel Gabriel. The first buildings were temporary and were made of willow poles and tules. In 1775, the mission was moved to higher ground to avoid flooding from the San Gabriel River. The present church was begun in 1791 and completed in 1805. It was damaged by the earthquakes of 1812, and it was repaired in 1828. The vaulted roof was replaced by a flat roof. The side wall is the real façade. The capped buttresses and the long narrow windows are not found in any other California Mission. The designs are believed to be traced to the Cathedral of Cordova, Spain, where the padre who designed San Gabriel received his training. During the period of 1818–1822, the padres donated seven barrels of brandy to help establish a chapel for the small, isolated pueblo of Los Angeles, nine miles away. The Church of Our Lady of Angeles still stands in downtown Los Angeles. It is known as the Plaza Church because it is near the plaza of El Pueblo de Los Angeles at the southern end of Olvera Street. Mission San Gabriel had the largest number of crops of any mission. It sat on three well-traveled trails: two from Mexico to Alta California and one from the East Coast of the United States to California. In 1987, an earthquake devastated the mission and it was closed until repairs were made. The mission is on Mission Drive in San Gabriel, nine miles east of downtown Los Angeles.

5. San Luis Obispo de Tolosa. Founded by Fr. Junipero Serra on September 1, 1772, and named for Saint Louis, Bishop

of Toulouse, France. The present building was constructed from 1792 to 1794. It has a belfry and vestibule combination that is unique among the missions. Three bells hang from openings directly above the church entrance. The bells are original. They were cast in Lima, Peru in 1818, and recast in Lima in 1878. Earthquakes damaged the belfry-vestibule in 1832 and 1868. The walls of the mission were once red. In 1876, the church was modernized with wooden siding and the ceiling was covered with tongue and groove sheathing. In 1880, the entire face of the mission was boarded over, and a New England steeple was added. In March 1920, a fire gutted the sacristy, and in 1930 a fire destroyed the convent. In 1934, the church was restored to its original form. The mission was restored in 1948. It is at 782 Monterey Street in San Luis Obispo.

6. San Francisco de Asis. Founded by Fr. Francisco Palou in 1776. On June 29, he celebrated Mass in a brushwood shelter, but on October 9, a wooden church plastered with mud and roofed with tules was ready. The present church was begun on April 25, 1782, and moved to a more favorable site. It was dedicated on April 3, 1791, and named for Saint Francis of Assisi, founder of the Franciscan Order, but it has always been known as Mission Dolores because the first site was alongside a stream named Arroyo de Las Dolores, for Our Lady of Sorrows. The church is the oldest intact building in San Francisco. As the population of San Francisco exploded following the Gold Rush, the church became too small to serve the parish, so a large church was built alongside it. It was

dedicated in 1876 on the 100th anniversary of the mission's founding. The 1906 earthquake spared Mission Dolores, but it damaged the new church so extensively that it had to be dismantled. A temporary wooden church served the parish until the ruined church was replaced in 1918 when it was dedicated at Christmas. Its architectural style was influenced by designs used at the San Diego exposition of 1915, and it towered over the mission chapel. In 1952, Pope Pius XII designated it a minor basilica because of its historic importance. It is at 3321 16th Street, San Francisco.

7. San Juan Capistrano. Founded twice, first on October 30, 1775, by Fr. Fermin Lasuen. Work stopped a week later when news arrived of an Indian attack at Mission San Diego. It was founded a second time on November 1, 1776, by Fr. Junipero Serra, and named for Saint John of Capistrano, Italy. On December 8, 1812, during Mass on the feast of the Immaculate Conception, an earthquake destroyed the church. The walls swayed back and forth dumping the massive concrete ceiling on the congregation. Forty Indian worshipers were crushed to death. The mission is one of only two still standing where it is known that Fr. Serra celebrated Mass. The other one is Mission Dolores. Pope John Paul II designated the mission a minor basilica in 2001. It is on Interstate 5 in San Juan Capistrano, sixty-five miles north of San Diego.

8. Santa Clara de Asis. Founded by Fr. Junipero Serra on January 12, 1777, and named for Saint Clare of Assisi, founder of the Order of Nuns called the Poor Clares. The first two

churches were built of logs in 1777 and 1779. The third church was made of adobe and was 100 feet long with four feet thick walls. It was completed in 1784, but an earthquake destroyed it in 1818. A temporary church was built until the fifth site and church was completed in 1825. Previous sites were moved because a series of floods from the Guadalupe River menaced the mission buildings. In 1926, a fire reduced the church to ashes. It was rebuilt in 1929. It is at 500 El Camino Real, Santa Clara, on the Santa Clara University campus and it serves as the chapel for the University.

9. San Buenaventura. Founded by Fr. Junipero Serra on March 31, 1782, and named for Saint Bonaventure. The first church burned down within ten years, and a new large one made of stone was dedicated in 1809, but earthquakes in 1812 damaged it severely. It was reconstructed in 1816. The mission is the only one known to have wooden bells. They were carved out of blocks two feet thick. They may have been used during Holy Week when metal bells were normally silent. They are on display in the mission museum. The mission was restored in 1957. It is at 211 Main Street, Ventura, east of U.S. Highway 101.

10. Santa Barbara. Founded by Fr. Fermin Lasuen on December 4, 1786, and named for Saint Barbara, a third century Roman martyr. The first mission buildings, started in 1787, were made of logs, brush and mud. As the Indian population grew, three churches were built, each larger than the previous one. The third one, built in 1794 was destroyed by

the earthquakes of 1812. The present church, made of stone, was begun in 1815 and dedicated on September 10, 1820. It is 161 feet long, forty-two feet high and twenty-seven feet wide. It had one tower, but a second tower was added in 1833, making it the only California Mission today with two similar towers. The façade was copied from the design of a Roman temple in 27 B.C., in an illustrated book by Vitruvius Polion, a Roman architect. In 1925, an earthquake nearly destroyed the church. The façade was rebuilt in 1950. The mission is at the end of Laguna Street in Santa Barbara.

11. La Purisima Conception. Founded by Fr. Fermin Lasuen on December 8, 1787, the feast of the Immaculate Conception. It was named the Immaculate Conception of Mary Most Pure. It was begun in 1788 and completed in 1791. In 1812, earthquakes destroyed it. In 1815, construction began on a new mission five miles inland. It was completed in 1818 in a linear layout. It is the only mission not built in a quadrangle except for Mission San Rafael. In 1824, when news of an Indian attack at Mission Santa Ines reached La Purisima, Indians took control of the mission for almost a month. In a battle with soldiers, sixteen Indians were killed, many were wounded, and one soldier was killed and three were wounded. The state acquired the property in 1935 and on December 7, 1941, dedicated it as a State Historic Park. It is at 2295 Purisima Road, five miles east of Lompoc.

12. Santa Cruz. Founded August 28, 1791, by Fr. Fermin Lasuen. The name is Spanish for Holy Cross. The church

was begun in 1793 and dedicated in May 1794. It measured 112 feet by thirty feet with a vaulted roof thirty feet high. The quadrangle was completed in 1795. In its prime, the Indian population was 523, the lowest of all the missions. The first autopsy in California's medical history was performed at the mission in 1814 following the death of Fr. Quintana two years earlier. Seven Indians were charged with murder, and the Governor sentenced them to a severe flogging. The church tower fell in 1840, and the entire church collapsed following an earthquake in 1857. In 1858, a frame church was built and it served until 1889 when it was replaced by the present white-painted brick church. In 1931, a replica of the mission church, about one-third the size of the original was built as a memorial chapel. It is on Emmet and School Streets in Santa Cruz.

13. Nuestra Señora de La Soledad. Founded October 9, 1771, by Fr. Fermin Lasuen, and dedicated to Our Lady of Solitude. The first church, a thatch roofed adobe was built in 1797 and enlarged in 1805. Jose Joaquin de Arrillaga, the first Spanish governor of Alta California, is buried at the mission. The chapel was rebuilt at least twice when the Salinas River flooded. The present chapel was built in 1832. The chapel and one wing were restored in 1954. The mission is one mile west of U.S. Highway 101, three miles west of Soledad.

14. San Jose. Founded by Fr. Fermin Lasuen on June 11, 1797, and named for Saint Joseph. The first church was begun in 1805 and dedicated on April 22, 1809. On October 21, 1868, it was destroyed by an earthquake. It was partly restored in 1916

and 1950. Robert Livermore, for whom the city and valley were named, is buried near the sanctuary of the church. From 1982 to 1985, the church was reconstructed. It is at 43300 Mission Blvd., Fremont, off Interstate 680, fifteen miles northeast of San Jose.

15. San Juan Bautista. Founded by Fr. Fermin Lasuen on June 24, 1797, the feast day of Saint John the Baptist, in Spanish, San Juan Bautista. The mission was completed in 1798, but earthquakes destroyed it in 1800. Construction of the present church began in June 1803 and continued until June 1812. At seventy-two feet wide and 188 feet long, it is the largest of the mission churches, and the only one with three aisles, but in 1812 the padres filled in the open arched walls with adobe because they thought it would help support the heavy roof during an earthquake. When the restoration of the mission was completed in 1976 for the United States Bicentennial, all three aisles of the church were opened for the first time since 1812. In the 1860s, Fr. Rubio, the pastor, covered the ceiling and floor of the church with wooden siding and installed a New England steepled belfry. The steeple collapsed in a storm in 1915. The San Andreas Fault passes through the mission grounds. The 1906 earthquake knocked down one of the walls of the church. The mission faces the plaza of San Juan Bautista State Historic Park. The mission is not a part of the park, but it is a quiet reminder of days gone by. It is in San Juan Bautista, four miles south of U.S. Highway 101, seventeen miles north of Salinas.

16. San Miguel Arcangel. Founded July 25, 1797, by Fr. Fermin Lasuen, and named for Saint Michael the Arcangel.

Two successive mud-roofed churches were used until 1806 when a fire consumed most of the buildings. The present church was begun in 1816 and completed in 1818. It is 144 feet long, twenty-seven feet wide and about forty feet high. On December 22, 2003, a 6.5 earthquake centered in San Simeon caused cracks on the façade of the church. It was closed to the public because of safety concerns while repairs were made. In September 2004, a smaller earthquake hit the region and the entire mission was closed to the public. It reopened on September 29, 2009. The mission is on old U.S. Highway 101 in San Miguel, ten miles north of Paso Robles.

17. San Fernando de España. Founded September 8, 1797, by Fr. Fermin Lasuen, and named for Saint Ferdinand, King of Spain. The first church was completed in 1799 but was replaced by a new church in 1800. In 1806, the first permanent church was completed, but it was damaged by earthquakes in 1812. Repairs were made, but vandals despoiled the mission and over time it collapsed. The only building remaining was the convento, a two-story padres quarters completed in 1822 that branched off the quadrangle. It is 243 feet long, sixty-five feet wide and forty-five feet high, the largest adobe structure in California. Today, it houses one of the oldest libraries in California. The fountain is in the shape of a Moorish star. It is original and is a copy of one in Cordova, Spain. On February 9, 1971, the Sylmar earthquake damaged the church beyond repair, and it had to be demolished and completely rebuilt. In 1974, an exact replica of the original church was dedicated.

On September 13, 1981, Cardinal Timothy Manning of the Archdiocese of Los Angeles dedicated a new Archival Center at San Fernando Mission. The function of the center is to collect, preserve and study documents associated with California's Catholic heritage. It is available to researchers by appointment. The mission is 1-1/2 miles west of San Fernando, off Interstate 5, on San Fernando Mission Blvd.

18.   San Luis Rey de Francia. Founded June 13, 1798, by Fr. Fermin Lasuen, and named for King Louis IX of France. The first adobe church was built in 1802. The present church was begun in 1811 and dedicated in 1815. It is 138 feet long. It is the only mission church with a wooden dome. It was built from pine wood brought down from Palomar Mountain. The mission occupies six acres of land, the largest in area of all the missions, and it served the largest Indian population of all the missions, more than 2,700 at one time. The livestock numbered more than 50,000. The mission was abandoned from 1865 to 1892 and fell into ruins. In 1893, restoration began and the mission was rededicated. It is on Mission Ave. in San Luis Rey, east of Oceanside.

In 1815, Mission San Luis Rey established San Antonio de Pala as an outpost, or asistencia, twenty miles to the east in the village of Pala. Pala was never granted mission status but at its peak of production it served 1,000 Indians, and its agricultural output surpassed some of the missions. San Antonio de Pala is the only surviving asistencia, and the chapel is the only one still being used by the Indians.

19. Santa Ines. Founded September 17, 1804, by Fr. Estevan Tapis, and named for Saint Agnes. The original church was built between 1805 and 1812, but earthquakes that year destroyed it. Rebuilding began in 1813 and the new church was dedicated in 1817. In 1824, as a result of harsh treatment by the military at the mission, an Indian revolt resulted in the deaths of two Indians, and in fires which destroyed part of the church. In 1904, Fr. Alexander Buckler, new pastor of the mission, with the aid of his niece, Marnie Goulet, began a twenty-year job of restoring the mission. Most of the restoration was completed in 1947 when the Hearst Foundation donated money for the project. The mission is at 1760 Mission Drive in Solvang.

20. San Rafael Arcangel. Named for Saint Rafael the Arcangel, whose name means "healing power of god." Founded December 14, 1817, by Fr. Vicente Sarria as a convalescent hospital for the Indian population at Mission Dolores, because of the serious mortality rate there attributed to the damp climate. San Rafael was founded as an asistencia of Mission Dolores, and the Indians were counted as part of the Mission Dolores population. Hundreds were sent there to recuperate in the sunshine. The church was built in 1818, but because of its function it was not built in the traditional quadrangle. It was granted mission status in October 1822, but it was abandoned in 1842 and torn down in 1870. A replica was built in 1949 with a star-shaped window like the one at Carmel Mission, and a bell hung from cross beams instead

of a bell tower. It is at 1104 Fifth Avenue in San Rafael, fifteen miles north of San Francisco.

21. San Francisco Solano. Named for Saint Francis Solano, a missionary to Peruvian Indians. Founded July 4, 1823, by Fr. Jose Altimira, without approval of the father-president of the missions. Approval was ultimately granted, and a whitewashed wooden church was dedicated in 1824. It was the only mission founded during California's Mexican period. A larger church was built in 1827 but torn down in 1838. In 1841, a small adobe church was built on the site of the original wooden structure. It served briefly as a parish church, but by 1881 it was too dilapidated to salvage, so a new church was built in another part of Sonoma. The 1906 earthquake damaged the church. The state repaired it from 1911 to 1913. Further restoration took place from 1943 to 1944. The mission is now part of Sonoma Mission State Historic Park. It is at 20 E. Spain Street in Sonoma.

NOTES

Chapter 1
A Forty-Nine Year Visit

1. Harry Downie honored (n.p.), April 22, 1971.
2. Celeste Pagliarulo S.N.D. de N., *Harry Downie and the Restoration of Mission San Carlos Borromeo 1931–1967*, p. 22, Los Angeles, California 2004.
3. *Cornerstone*, Newsletter of the Carmel Mission Foundation, Fall 2011.
4. Helen Hunt Jackson, *Glimpses of California and the Missions*, p. 47, Boston, Little, Brown & Company, 1903.
5. Elsie Martinez, *What's Doing*, October 1946, "Almost Two Centuries: The Story of Father Serra's Own Mission."
6. Robert Louis Stevenson, *The Old Pacific Capital, Monterey*, 1880.
7. Monterey Peninsula Herald, September 30, 1964, "San Carlos Fiesta Revived at Mission."
8. The Monterey Californian, "San Carlos Day," "A Barbarian at the Carmello Mission," November 11, 1879.
9. Sydney Temple, *The Carmel Mission*, p. 159, Western Tanager Press, Santa Cruz, California, 1980.
10. Miriam Downie, Harry's daughter, interview by author, Carmel, California.

11 Newspaper clipping in Sir Harry Downie Museum.
12 See note no. 10.
13 See note no. 2, p. 2.
14 Msgr. Francis J. Weber, *The Observer*, Monterey, California, December 22, 1982.
15 "Harry Downie – Memories 3," p. 2.
16 See note no. 2, p. 1.

Chapter 2
Boyhood Memories

17 "Harry Downie – Memories 3," p. 1.
18 Miriam Downie, Harry's daughter, interview by author, Carmel, California.
19 Gregory Lee, "California Missions," p. 41, *A Guide to the State's Spanish Heritage*, American Travelers Press, Phoenix, 1952.
20 James D. Hart, *A Companion to California*, pp. 464 and 465, New York University Press, 1978.
21 Celeste Pagliarulo S.N.D. de N., *Harry Downie and the Restoration of Mission San Carlos Borromeo 1931–1967*, p. 1, Los Angeles, California, 2004.
22 See note no. 18.
23 See note no. 21.
24 "San Francisco de Asis," p. 146, *The California Missions*, Sunset Books, Inc., Menlo Park, California, 1979.
25 "Harry Downie and Mission Dolores," p. 5.
26 Doris Muscatine, *Old San Francisco: The Biography of a City*, pp. 428–436, Putnam & Sons, New York.

27 See note no. 25.
28 See note no. 24, pp. 139 & 141.
29 David J. McLaughlin and Dr. Ruben G. Mendoza, Contributing Editor, *The California Missions Source Book*, p. 33, University of New Mexico Press, 2009.
30 See note no. 24, pp. 145–147.
31 "Harry Downie and Mission Dolores 1," p. 10.
32 Tim Appenzeller, "Tracking the Next Killer Flu," *National Geographic*, October 2005, pp. 2–31.
33 "Harry Downie and Mission Dolores," p. 6.
34 Ibid.
35 Celeste Pagliarulo S.N.D. de N., *Harry Downie and the Restoration of Mission San Carlos Borromeo 1931–1967*, p. 2, Los Angeles, California, 2004.
36 Bruce Walter Barton, *The Tree at the Center of the World*, Ross-Erickson Publishers, Inc., Santa Barbara, 1980.

Chapter 3
A One-Man Crew

37 Celeste Pagliarulo, S.N.D. de N., *Harry Downie and the Restoration of Mission San Carlos Borromeo 1931–1967*, pp. 17 & 18, Los Angeles, California, 2004.
38 Bruna Odello, interview by author, Carmel, California.
39 Ibid.
40 "Harry Downie – Memories 3" p. 6.
41 See note no. 37, p. 18.
42 See note no. 37, p. 19.
43 Rev. Pacificus Kennedy O.F.M., "Sir Harry Downie: A

Medieval Man," publication unknown, December 13, 1964, 44 See note no. 37, p. 24.
45 Miriam Downie, Harry's daughter, interview by author, Carmel, California.
46 Ibid.
47 Ibid.
48 Msgr. Francis J. Weber, interview by author, San Fernando, California.
49 "Memories 2," pp. 2–3.
50 "Carmel Mission," pp. 15–16.
51 Booklet, *The Story of the Father Junipero Serra Memorial Cenotaph in the Mission San Carlos Borromeo de Carmelo*, Carmel, California, Carmel Mission Basilica, 2006.
52 Sydney Temple, *The Carmel Mission*, p. 123, Western Tanager Press, Santa Cruz, California, 1980.
53 *Central California Register*, "Restorer of the Missions," Friday, August 17, 1951.
54 See note no. 37, pp. 2 & 16.
55 Kristina Foss, telephone interview by author, Santa Barbara, California.

Chapter 4
A Note in a Bottle

56 "Last Outposts of Empire," p. 39, *The California Missions*, Sunset Books, Inc., Menlo Park, California, 1979.
57 Msgr. Francis J. Weber, *The Life and Times of Fray Junipero Serra*, p. 25, EZ Nature Books, P.O. Box 4206, San Luis Obispo, California, 1988.

58 "San Diego de Alcala," pp. 71–72, *The California Missions,* Sunset Books, Inc., Menlo Park, California, 1979.
59 "San Diego de Alcala," p. 74–75, *The California Missions,"* Sunset Books, Inc., Menlo Park, California, 1979.
60 "Portola Cross," p. 4.
61 James Culleton, *Indians and Pioneers of Old Monterey,* p. 33, Academy of California Church History, Fresno, California, 1950.
62 "Portola Cross," pp. 4–5.
63 Robert W. Reese, *A Brief History of Old Monterey,* p. 15, City of Monterey Planning Commission, December 1969.
64 See note no. 61, p. 36.
65 "Portola Cross," p. 5.
66 See note no. 61, p. 37.

Chapter 5
Mission San Carlos Borromeo

67 Athanasius Schaefer, "San Carlos de Borromeo de Carmelo," p.1of6, http//www.athanasius.com/camission/carmel.htm, 11-5-2010.
68 James Culleton, *Indians and Pioneers of Old Monterey,* pp. 39–40, Academy of California Church History, Fresno, California, 1950.
69 Ibid, p. 42.
70 Frances Rand Smith, *The Architectural History of Mission San Carlos Borromeo,* p. 18, published by the California Historical Commission, Berkeley, 1921.

71 See note no. 68, p. 50.
72 David Paul Elder, *The Old Spanish Missions of California*, p. 11, Paul Elder and Company, Publishers, San Francisco, 1913.
73 *Monterey Trader*, "Calle De Alvarado," August 22, 1935, Archives, Monterey Public Library.
74 Samuel L. Wright, Jr., "The Bells of the Carmel Mission," Printed by Print Pelican, 2010.
75 See note no. 70, p. 51.
76 Helen Hunt Jackson, *Glimpses of California and the Missions*, p. 43, Boston: Little, Brown & Co. 1903.
77 Monterey/San Carlos Church, p. 2.
78 "San Carlos Cathedral, the Royal Presidio Chapel," Parish News.

Chapter 6
The Birthplace of California

79 "Portola Cross," p. 2.
80 Donald Thomas Clark, *Monterey County Place Names: A Geographical Dictionary*, pp. 415–416, Kestrel Press, Carmel Valley, California, 1991.
81 *Monterey Peninsula Herald*, "Citizens Act Without Officials Permission," "Redwood Cross Returns to Carmel Meadows Area," Wednesday, January 11, 1984.
82 *Monterey Peninsula Herald*, "Portola-Crespi Cross Dedicated at Rites, Bicentennial Launched," Wednesday, December 10, 1969.
83 *The Herald*, "Wooden Cross at Beach Cut Down," Monday, September 21, 2009.

84 *Monterey Peninsula Herald,* "For Bicentennial: Stamp to Depict Carmel Mission" (n.d.).

Chapter 7
Our Lady of Bethlehem

85 "Our Lady of Belen and the Reredos," pp. 1–2.
86 *Monterey Peninsula Herald,* "70,000 Catholic Pilgrims to Converge on Carmel Mission in May," Monday, February 8, 1954.
87 See note no. 86.
88 *Monterey Peninsula Herald,* "Old Statue Comes Home on Christmas Eve," December 18, 1945.
89 See note no. 85, p. 4.
90 See note no. 86.

Chapter 8
Captain of the Indians

91 "Carmel Mission," pp. 4 & 12.
92 Ibid, p. 11.
93 *The Pine Cone,* Carmel-by-the-Sea, California, August 24, 1972, "Carmel Closeup Harry Downie He brings history to life," by Judith A. Eisner.
94 Celeste Pagliarulo, S.N.D. de N., *Harry Downie and the Restoration of Mission San Carlos Borromeo 1931–1967,* p. 10, Los Angeles, California, 2004.
95 "Memories 2," p. 4.

96   *Monterey Peninsula Herald,* "Carmel Mission Fiesta is Grand Success October 3, 1964."
97   "Carmel Indians," p. 9.

Chapter 9
A Year of Earthquakes

98   Hubert Howe Bancroft, *History of California Volume II 1801–1824,* p. 200, The History Company, Publishers, San Francisco, 1886.
99   *The California Missions,* "San Juan Capistrano," pp. 155–156, Sunset Books, Inc., Menlo Park, California, 1979.
100 David Paul Elder, *The Old Spanish Missions of California,* p. 47, Paul Elder and Company, Publishers, San Francisco, 1913.
101 *Supplement to The Observer,* March 12, 1980, *Carmel Closeup* "Harry Downie He Brings History to Life," Judith A. Eisner.
102 *The Herald Weekend Magazine,* September 16, 1972, "Art Treasures Get Loving Care at Carmel Mission."
103 *The California Missions,* "Acknowledgments," no page number, Sunset Books, Inc., Menlo Park, California, 1979.
104 Rev. Pacificus Kennedy O.F.M., "Sir Harry Downie: A Medieval Man," publication unknown, December 13, 1964.
105 *Game & Gossip,* "Harry Downie: A Dedicated Man," p. 26, December 1963, by Helen Spangenberg
106 "Carmel Mission," p. 13.

107 Celeste Pagliarulo, S.N.D. de N., *Harry Downie and the Restoration of Mission San Carlos Borromeo 1931–1967*, p. 45, note no. 110, Los Angeles, California, 2004.
108 *Supplement to The Observer*, March 12, 1980, "California's First Library," *Harry J. Downie, Curator Carmel Mission*, previously published October 25, 1966.
109 *Monterey Peninsula Herald*, "Carmel Mission Bible to be Used by Reagan," December 28, 1969.

Chapter 10
The Founder of California

110 Msgr. Francis J. Weber, *The Life and Times of Fray Junipero Serra*, pp. 1 & 4, EZ Nature Books, P.O. 4206, San Luis Obispo, CA 93403, 1988.
111 Ibid, p. 5.
112 "Portola Cross," pp. 11–12.
113 *The California Missions*, "Founders of the Missions," pp. 310–311, Sunset Books, Inc., Menlo Park, California, 1979.
114 *PG&E Progress (n.d.)*, 245 Market Street, *Mission Padre:* "Junipero Serra Launched State a Farm, Economic Empire."
115 Martin J. Morgado, *Junipero Serra, a Pictorial Biography*, photo No. 136, Siempre Adelante Publishing, 1190 Alta Vista Road, Monterey, California 93940, 1991.
116 See note no. 111, p. 52.
117 *Siempre Adelante!* Spring/Summer 2007, The Newsletter for the Cause of Blessed Junipero Serra; address on Father

Junipero Serra and Evangelization: Homily at the Carmel Mission Basilica by Pope John Paul II, September 17, 1987.
118 Fr. Zephyrn Englehardt O.F.M., *Mission San Carlos Borromeo The Father of the Missions*, p. 101, Ballena Presss, P.O. Box 711, Ramona, California 92065, 1973.
119 "Mission Carmel's Seven Churches, No. 5, Serra Adobe Church 1783–93," Timeline in Carmel Mission Basilica Museum.
120 TIME *The Weekly News Magazine*, "Sainthood for Serra?" September 6, 1937.
121 Rev. Pacificus Kennedy O.F.M., "Sir Harry Downie: A Medieval Man," publication unknown, December 13, 1964.
122 Pamphlet – *Junipero Serra, Illustrated Timeline of Junipero Serra's Life*, Pentacle Press, 2005.
123 Martin J. Morgado, *Junipero Serra, a Pictorial Biography*, p. 96, Siempre Adelante Publishing, Monterey, California, 1991.

Chapter 11
A Papal Visit

124 Celeste Pagliarulo, S.N.D. de N., *Harry Downie and the Restoration of Mission San Carlos Borromeo 1931–1937*, pp. 24–25, Los Angeles, California, 2004.
125 *Monterey Peninsula Herald*, "Father Serra Would Like Mission School," October 23, 1945.
126 See note no. 124, p. 25.
127 *Monterey Peninsula Herald*, "Bing Starts the Ball Rolling New Carmel Mission Project Launched," Thursday, July 15, 1950.

128 "Memories 2," p. 7.
129 See note no. 125.
130 *Monterey Peninsula Herald*, "New Carmel Mission Chapel Completed" (n.d.).
131 See note no. 124, pp. 25–26.
132 "Our Lady of Belen and the Reredos," p. 6.
133 Bayard Taylor, *Eldorado or Adventures in the Path of Empire,* p. 131, New York: Alfred A. Knopf, 1949.
134 Celeste Pagliarulo, S.N.D. de N., *Harry Downie and the Contents of Mission San Carlos Borromeo 1931–1967,* p. 6, Friends of the Archival Center, Los Angeles, 2004.
135 T. M. LeBerthon, "Restorer of the Missions," *Central California Register,* Friday, August 17, 1951.
136 See note no. 134.
137 See note no. 134, p. 9.
138 Miriam Downie, Harry's daughter, interview by author, Carmel, California.
139 Siempre *Adelante,* The Newsletter for the Cause of Blessed Junipero Serra, Spring/Summer 2007; address on Father Junipero Serra and Evangelization: Homily at the Carmel Mission Basilica by Pope John Paul II, September 17, 1987.

Chapter 12
A Steak in the Freezer

140 Sister Francisca, interview by author, Carmelite Monastery near Carmel, California.
141 Rui Barcelos, interview by author, Monterey, California.

142 Edward Soberanes, telephone interview by author, Carmel, California.
143 Huu Van Nguyen, interview by author, Carmel, California.
144 Emmett O'Boyle, interview by author, Salinas, California.
145 Pat Hathaway, interview by author, Monterey, California.
146 *Salinas Californian, Valley Today*, Tuesday, June 3, 1980, "Downie's Aide Takes Over," Linda Lewis.
147 *The Herald*, Wednesday, December 25, 2013, "Looking Back on a Special Mission."
148 Robert Morton, interview by author, Pleasant Hill, California.
149 Ibid.
150 Ibid.
151 Ibid.
152 See note no. 147.
153 See note no. 147.
154 See note no. 147.

Chapter 13
Secularization

155 *The California Missions*, "Material and Spiritual Profile of the Missions," p. 316, Sunset Books, Inc., Menlo Park, California, 1979.
156 San Antonio de Pala, p. 284, The California Missions Sunset Books, Inc., Menlo Park, California, 1979.
157 James Culleton, *Indians and Pioneers of Old Monterey*, p. 181, Academy of California Church History, Fresno, California, 1950.

158 James D. Hart, *A Companion to California*, p. 146, New York, Oxford University Press, 1978.
159 Rev. Gerald J. Geary A.M., *Secularization of the California Missions*, The Catholic University of America, Washington, D.C., 1934, pp. 55, 56 & 78.
160 William H. Beezley, and David E. Torey, Editors, *Viva Mexico! Viva La Independencia! Celebrations of September 16*, Scholarly Resources, Inc., Wilmington, DE, 2001.
161 See note no. 159, pp. 149, 151, 152, & 171–173.
162 Richard Henry Dana, Jr., *Two Years Before the Mast*, pp. 172 & 173, published by The Classics Club, by Walter J. Black, New York.
163 "The Disaster of Secularization," p. 66, *The California Missions*, Sunset Books, Inc., Menlo Park, California, 1979.

Chapter 14
Restorations

164 "Mission San Luis Obispo," p. 1.
165 *San Luis Obispo Telegram-Tribune*, "Renovations of the Mission have revealed many things" (n.d.).
166 *The California Missions*, "San Luis Obispo de Tolosa," pp. 134 & 136, Sunset Books, Inc., Menlo Park, California, 1979.
167 See note no., 162, p 4.
168 Ibid.
169 See note no., 162, pp. 2, 3 & 6.
170 *The Herald*, "Hotel Wasn't Luxury for Pilot Trainees," May 16, 2011.

171 See note no. 162, pp. 1, 2 & 6.
172 San Luis Obispo Telegram-Tribune, "Restoration offers clues about Mission" (n.d.).
173 See note no. 162, p.4.
174 "Mission San Antonio," pp. 1, 2 & 7.
175 See note no. 172, pp. 1 & 4.
176 Beatrice (Tid) Casey, *Padres and People of Old Mission San Antonio*, p. 49, published by The King City Rustler-Herald, King City, California, May 1957.
177 See note no. 172, pp. 1 & 4.
178 See note no. 172, p, 2.
179 Pamphlet, "Mission San Antonio de Padua."
180 Ibid.
181 Ibid.
182 See note no. 174 p. 51.
183 See note no. 172, pp. 4–5.
184 See note no. 172, p. 8.
185 See note no. 172, p. 2.
186 Ibid.
187 Miriam Downie, Harry's daughter, interview by author, Carmel, California.
188 "San Antonio de Padua," *The California Missions*, p. 101, Sunset Books, Inc., Menlo Park, California, 1979.
189 *Mission Bell*, newsletter of the *Campaign for the Preservation of Mission San Antonio de Padu*, Vol. 3, No. 2, Summer 2014.
190 "San Juan Bautista: Beneath a sleepy little town lies a bedrock of state history," *Alta Vista Gallery, The Sunday Magazine of the Monterey County Herald*, June 22, 1997.

191 "San Juan Bautista – a visit to yesterday," *The Sunday Peninsula Herald, Weekend Magazine,* July 19, 1981.
192 Martha Lowman, *California's Mission San Juan Bautista,* p. 4, produced by Hubert A. Lowman, 11015 Bobcat Lane, Arroyo Grande, California 93420.
193 See note no. 189.
194 "San Juan Bautista," pp. 246 & 253, *The California Missions,* Sunset Books, Inc., Menlo Park, California, 1979.
195 See note no. 190, p. 16.
196 See note no. 189.
197 Ibid.
198 Helen Hunt Jackson, *Glimpses of California and the Missions,* p. 94, Boston: Little, Brown & Company, 1903.
199 Cassette tape. Harry Downie, Recollections of the restoration of Mission Soledad.
200 John Billman, "Harry Downie: The Man Who Restored the Missions," *Monterey Life,* pp. 31–33, August 1980.
201 Rev. Francis J. Weber "Harry Downie – Living Legend," *The Monitor,* San Francisco, California, April 3, 1964.
202 Miriam Downie, Harry's daughter, interview by author, Carmel, California.
203 Msgr. Francis J. Weber, correspondence with author, November 2, 2009.
204 Ibid.

Chapter 15
An American da Vinci

205 "Portola Cross," p. 3.

206 Harry Downie honored (n.p.), April 22, 1971.
207 *Monterey Peninsula Herald,* "Downie Still at Work – Dedicated to Historical Integrity," December 14, 1967.
208 *Monterey Peninsula Herald,* "Carmel Mission Restoration, 700 Honor Priest, Layman for Work at Carmelo Borromeo," January 12, 1955.
209 "Our Lady of Belen and the Reredos," p. 4.
210 *Noticias de Puerto de Monterey,* A Quarterly Bulletin of Historic Monterey Issued by the Monterey History and Art Association, Vol. XXV, No. 1, March 1982, REBUILDER OF MISSIONS: Henry John "Harry" Downie 1903–1980.
211 See note no. 204.
212 Msgr. Francis J. Weber, interview by author, San Fernando, California.
213 Celeste Pagliarulo, S.N.D. de N., *Harry Downie and the Contents of Mission San Carlos Borromeo 1931–1967,* p. 25, Endnote No. 54, Friends of the Archival Center, Los Angeles, 2005.
214 See note no. 210.
215 Memo from Professor Robert Kirchner of Fresno Pacific University.
216 *The Pine Cone,* Carmel-by-the-Sea, California, "Harry Downie has a Soft Heart and a Hard Head," August 31, 1972.
217 *The Herald Weekend Magazine,* September 16, 1972, "Art Treasures Get Loving Care at Carmel Mission."
218 *The Herald,* Thursday, January 5, 2012, "Archaeologist Aids Stamp Design."

Chapter 16
A Remarkable Man

219 "Carmel Mission," p. 6.
220 Letter from Timothy Cardinal Manning, Archbishop of Los Angeles, dated March 12, 1980, on the passing of Harry Downie.
221 *Monterey Peninsula Herald*, "Harry Downie, Carmel Mission Restorer Dies," March 10, 1980.
222 Letter dated March 10, 1980 to Harry Downie from Orinda Giannini Petty, Past President of N.D.G.W.
223 Congressional Record – House 96th Congress, Second Session, Tuesday, July 1, 1980, H. Doc No. 111, "Harry Downie: Bringing History to Life," Mr. Panetta.
224 Pamphlet: "The Mass and Dedication of the Harry Downie Museum."
225 Nietzsche, Friedrich Wilhelm, "Human, All Too Human," 1878.
226 "Eulogy Given by Father Farrell," transcribed by Celeste Pagliarulo, S.N.D. de N., April–May 2003, from a tape recording of Father Lawrence Farrell on March 13, 1980, at Mission San Carlos Borromeo Basilica.

BIBLIOGRAPHY

Harry Downie was interviewed frequently at Carmel Mission from October 1973 through 1974. The Most Reverend Harry Anselm Clinch, Bishop of the Diocese, wanted a record of Harry's encyclopedic knowledge of the California Missions and of his work restoring some of them. The tape-recorded interviews were subsequently transcribed onto hard copy and categorized by subject. Harry's daughter Miriam gave copies to the author, who referred to them extensively in addition to the other listed sources. Included among the interviews are two interviews of Harry in 1978 by Professor Robert Kirchner of Fresno Pacific University, while he was on field trips to Carmel Mission with his students, and one interview of Harry with a colleague in 1979. Professor Kirchner gave the author written authorization to use information from the interviews for publication, and to use a student's response to an essay question about Harry Downie. The interview subjects are:

Memories 1
Memories 2
Harry Downie – Memories 3
Carmel Mission
Harry Downie and Mission Dolores 1
Carmel Indians

Foundation and Growth
Portola Cross
Construction Techniques
Our Lady of Belen and the Reredos
Exhumation of 1943
Monterey/San Carlos Church
Mission San Luis Obispo
Mission Santa Cruz
Mission San Antonio
Harry Downie and Mission Dolores
Monterey County Missions
Eulogy Given by Father Farrell

PUBLISHED SOURCES

Appenzeller, Tim. "Tracking the Next Killer Flu." *National Geographic*, October 2005, pp. 2–31.

Ayres, Diana. "The Cause of Father Serra." *What's Doing*, June 1949, Vol. 3, No. 12, p. 7.

Bancroft, Hubert Howe. *History of California Volume II 1801–1824*. The History Company, Publishers, 1886.

Barry, John M. *The Great Influenza*. Viking Penguin, New York, 2004.

Bartlett, John M. *Bartlett's Familiar Quotations*, Fourteenth Edition, Little, Brown and Company, 1968.

Barton, Bruce Walter. *The Tree at 'The Center of the World.'* Ross-Erikson Publishers, Inc., Santa Barbara, 1980.

Beezley, William H. and David E. Torey, Editors, *Viva Mexico! Viva La Independencia! Celebrations of September 16*, Scholarly Resources, Inc., Wilmington, DE, 2001.

Billman, John. "Harry Downie: The Man Who Restored the Missions." *Monterey Life*, August 1980, pp. 31–33.

California Historical Landmarks, Office of Historic Preservation, California State Parks, Sacramento, California, 1996.

Carmel Mission Docent Association. *God Leads Me, The Huu Van Nguyen Story, A Testimony of Faith*, published in honor of Huu Van Nguyen, 2014.

Casey, Beatrice. *Padres and People of Old Mission San Antonio*, published by The Rustler-Herald, King City, California, May 1957.

Clark, Donald Thomas. *Monterey County Place Names: A Geographical Dictionary*. Krestel Press: Carmel Valley, California, 1991.

Culleton, James. *Indians and Pioneers of Old Monterey*. Academy of California Church History, Fresno, California, 1950.

Dana, Richard Henry, Jr. *Two Years Before the Mast*, pp. 172–173, published for The Classics Club, by Walter J. Black, New York.

Edwards, Tryon, D.D. *The New Dictionary of Thoughts*, Standard Book Company, 1964.

Elder, David Paul. *The Old Spanish Missions of California*. Paul Elder and Company, Publishers, San Francisco, 1913.

Engelhardt, Fr. Zephryn O.F.M. *Mission San Carlos Borromeo the Father of the Missions*, Ballena Press, P.O. Box 711, Ramona, California 92065, 1973.

Geary, Rev. Gerald J. A.M. *Secularization of the California Missions*. The Catholic University of America, Washington, D.C.

Geiger, Maynard Jr. *The Life and Times of Fray Junipero Serra, O.F.M.*, Washington, 1959.

Giordano, Albert G., Ph.D., KHS. *The Trilogy of the Life of Blessed Junipero Serra and the 21 California Missions*, Best Publishers, P.O. Box 3673, Carmel by the Sea, CA 93921.

Hackel, Steven W. *Junipero Serra, California's Founding Father*, Hill and Wang, New York, 2013.

Hamnett, Brian. *A Concise History of Mexico*. Cambridge University Press, 1999.

Hart, James D. *A Companion to California*. New York: Oxford University Press, 1978.

Iacopi, Robert. *Earthquake Country*. Lane Book Company, Menlo Park, California, 1964.

Jackson, Helen Hunt. *Glimpses of California and the Missions*. Boston: Little, Brown & Company, 1902.

Kocher, Paul H. *Mission San Luis Obispo de Tolosa: A Historical Sketch*. Blake Printing and Publishing, Inc., San Luis Obispo, California, 1972.

Kolata, Gina. *Flu: The Story of the Great Influenza Pandemic of 1918 and the Search for the Virus that Causes it*. Farrar, Straus and Giroux, New York, 1999.

Lee, Gregory. *California Missions: A Guide to the State's Spanish Heritage*. American Traveler Press, a Division of Primer Publishers, 5738 North Central Avenue, Phoenix, Arizona.

Leffingwell, Randy and Alastair Worden. *California Missions and Presidios*. Voyageur Press, Stillwater, MN, 2005.

Lowman, Martha H. *California's Mission San Juan Bautista*. Hubert A. Lowman, 11015 Bobcat Lane, Arroyo Grande, CA 93420.

McLaughlin, David J. and Dr. Ruben G. Mendoza, Contributing Editor, *The California Missions Source Book*.

Miller, Robert Ryal. *Mexico: A History*. University of Oklahoma Press, Norman, 1985.

Morgado, Martin J. *Junipero Serra, A Pictorial Biography*, Siempre Adelante Publishing, Monterey, California, 1991.

———, *Junipero Serra's Legacy*, published 1987 by Mount Carmel, P.O. Box 51326, Pacific Grove, CA 93950.

Muscatine, Doris. *Old San Francisco: The Biography of a City.* G. P. Putnam's Sons, New York, 1975.

Pagliarulo, Celeste, S.N.D. de N. *Harry Downie and the Restoration of Mission San Carlos Borromeo 1931–1937.* Los Angeles, California, 2004.

Pagliarulo, Celeste, S.N.D. de N. *Harry Downie and the Contents of Mission San Carlos Borromeo 1931–1967.* Friends of the Archival Center, Los Angeles, California, 2005.

Palou's Life of Fray Junipero Serra, translated by Rev. Maynard J. Geiger O.F.M. Reprinted with the permission of the Academy of American Franciscan History for the 200th anniversary of Serra's demise, August 28, 1984.

Pérouse, Jean Francois de la. *Life in a California Mission: Monterey in 1786,* Santa Clara University, Santa Clara, California, Heyday, Berkeley, California, 2007.

Reese, Robert W. *A Brief History of Old Monterey.* City of Monterey Planning Commission, December 1969.

Ruscin, Terry. *Mission Memoirs,* Sunbelt Publications, San Diego, California, 1999.

Shelton, Tamara Venit. "Unmasking Historic Spaces: Urban Progress and the San Francisco Cemetery Debate, 1895–1937." California History. *The Journal of the California Historical Society,* Volume 85, Number 3, 2008.

Slevin, L.S., and M.E. Slevin. *Guide Book to the Mission of San Carlos at Carmel and Monterey, California,* Carmel, California, 1912.

Smith, Frances Rand. *The Architectural History of Mission San Carlos Borromeo.* Published by the California Historical Commission, Berkeley, 1921.

Spangenberg, Helen. *Game & Gossip,* December 1963, "El Viejo."
Ibid. "Harry Downie: A Dedicated Man."
Stevens, Janice and Pat Hunter. *Remembering the California Missions,* published by Craven Street Books, an imprint of Linden Publishing, 2006 S. Mary, Fresno, California 93721, 2010.
Stevenson, Robert Louis. *The Old Pacific Capital Monterey 1880.*
Sunset Books, Inc. *The California Missions.* Menlo Park, California, 1979.
Taylor, Bayard. *Eldorado or Adventures in the Path of Empire.* New York, Alfred A. Knopf, 1949.
Temple, Sydney. *The Carmel Mission,* Western Tanager Press, Santa Cruz, California, 1980.
Time The Weekly News Magazine. "Sainthood for Serra?" September 6, 1937.
Via, "California Missions Saving Grace," pp. 24–31, November–December 2005.
Weber, Msgr. Francis J. *The Life and Times of Fray Junipero Serra.* EZ Nature Books, PO 4206, San Luis Obispo 93403, 1988.
———, *The Mission in the Valley,* Kimberly Press, Inc., Santa Barbara, California, 1995.
Wright, John W., Editor, *The New York Times 2008 Almanac,* 1133 Broadway, New York, NY 10010.
Wright, Samuel L., Jr. *The Bells of the Carmel Mission,* printed by Print Pelican, 2010.
Yenne, Bill. *The Missions of California,* Central Coast Press, San Luis Obispo, California 93403, 2009.

Periodicals and Letters

Monterey Peninsula Herald, December 29, 1943, "Body of Serra Exhumed, Reburied."

Monterey Peninsula Herald, October 23, 1945, "Father Serra Would Like Mission School."

Monterey Peninsula Herald, December 18, 1945, "Old Statue Comes Home on Christmas Eve."

What's Doing, October 1946, "Almost Two Centuries: The Story of Father Serra's Own Mission," Elsie Martinez.

Monterey Peninsula Herald, February 23, 1960, "Carmel Basilica: What It Means to Mission."

Monterey Peninsula Herald, December 28, 1969, "Carmel Mission Bible to be Used by Reagan."

The Sunday Herald, Sunday, June 22, 1966, "A Personal View of Carmel Mission."

The Herald, Saturday, April 15, 1989, "Carmel Mission's New Pastor Awed by Serra."

The Pine Cone, Carmel-by-the-Sea, California, August 24, 1972, "He Brings History to Life," Judith A. Eisner.

The Pine Cone, Carmel-by-the-Sea, California, August 31, 1972, "Harry Downie has a Soft Heart and a Hard Head."

The Monitor, San Francisco, April 3, 1964, "Harry Downie – Living Legend," Father Weber.

Monterey Peninsula Herald, Monday, October 12, 1964, Fiesta de San Carlos. Honor "El Capitan" at Nov. 1 Event.

Monterey Peninsula Herald, September 30, 1964, "San Carlos Fiesta Revived at Mission."

Monterey Peninsula Herald (n.d.), "Benefit for Carmel Mission."

Monterey Peninsula Herald, October 3, 1964, "Carmel Mission: Fiesta is Grand Success."

Monterey Peninsula Herald (n.d.), "For Bicentennial: Stamp to Depict Carmel Mission."

Monterey Peninsula Herald, Tuesday, September 20, 1966, "Carmel, 1879: RLS tells of Fiesta at Mission."

Monterey Peninsula Herald, Tuesday, October 18, 1966, "Carmel Mission Stands Once More as Serra Constructed it."

Monterey Peninsula Herald, Monday, May 10, 1965, "Carmel was the 'Jewel' in Fr. Serra's Chain of Franciscan Missions."

Monterey Peninsula Herald, Monday, March 23, 1964, "Easter at the Capital of Far West's Missions."

Ibid. "Fr. Serra, Founder of West's Missions, Buried at Carmel."

Monterey Peninsula Herald, December 14, 1967, "Dedicated to Historical Integrity: Downie Still at Work."

Monterey Peninsula Herald, Wednesday, December 10, 1969, "Portola-Crespi Cross Dedicated at Rites: Bicentennial Year Launched."

Monterey Peninsula Herald, January 12, 1955, "Carmel Mission Restoration: 700 to Honor Priest, Layman for Work at Carmelo Borromeo."

PG&E Progress, 245 Market Street, San Francisco 91106 (n.d.),

"Mission Padre: Junipero Serra Launched State as Farm, Economic Empire."

Central California Register, Friday, August 17, 1951, "Restorer of the Missions," T. M. LeBerthon.

Monterey Peninsula Herald, January 14, 1969, "Curator Downie Honored: A Community's Thanks."

Publication unknown, December 13, 1964, "Sir Harry Downie: A Medieval Man," Rev. Pacificus Kennedy O.F.M.

The Sunday Peninsula Herald, Sunday, March 9, 1975, "Peninsula Life: Saintly Faces of Mission Carmel."

San Jose Mercury, April 8, 1973, "Modern Man of the Missions," Sally Fisher, *California Today.*

Santa Cruz Sentinel, Sunday, May 18, 1980, "He Helped Preserve 'The Tree at the Center of the World.'"

Monterey Peninsula Herald, March 10, 1980, "Harry Downie Carmel Mission Restorer Dies."

Salinas Californian, Monday, July 7, 1980, "Men with a Mission: Downie Labor of Love Restored a Gem of Church," Linda Lewis.

The Observer, Monterey, California, January 20, 1982, "Junipero Serra: Bishops Urge Canonization."

The Observer, Monterey, California, December 22, 1982, "California's Catholic Heritage: The Downie Memorial," Msgr. Francis J. Weber.

Congressional Record – House 96th Congress, Second Session, Tuesday, July 1, 1980, H. Doc. No. 111, "Harry Downie: Bringing History to Life," Mr. Panetta.

Shirlie Stoddard, "Art Treasurers Get Loving Care at Carmel Mission: Restorer Harry Downie becomes an Archivist,"

The Sunday Peninsula Herald, Weekend Magazine, September 16, 1972.

John Billman, "San Juan Bautista – A Visit to Yesterday," *The Sunday Peninsula Herald, Weekend Magazine,* July 19, 1981.

John Billman, "San Juan Bautista," *Monterey Peninsula Herald, Gallery Magazine,* June 22, 1997.

Monterey Trader, August 22, 1935, "Calle De Alvarado."

Supplement to the Observer, March 12, 1980, "Carmel Closeup: "Harry Downie: He Brings History to Life," Judith A. Eisner.

Ibid. "California's First Library: Harry J. Downie Curator Carmel Mission," previously published October 25, 1966.

Eulogy Given by Father Farrell, transcribed by Celeste Paliarulo, S.N. D. de N., April–May 2003 from tape recording of Father Lawrence Farrell on March 13, 1980, at Mission San Carlos Borromeo Basilica.

Orinda, Giannini Petty, N.D.G.W., Letter to Harry Downie dated March 10, 1980, advising him he was to receive the California Historical Society award for Historic Preservation on March 16, 1980.

Timothy Cardinal Manning, Archbishop of Los Angeles, 1531 West Ninth Street, Los Angeles, California 90015, Statement issued March 12, 1980, upon the passing of Harry Downie, Curator of Carmel Mission Basilica.

Siempre Adelante! The Newsletter for the Cause of Blessed Junipero Serra, Spring/Summer 2007; address on Father Junipero Serra and Evangelization Homily at the Carmel

Mission Basilica by Pope John Paul II, September 17, 1987.

Pamphlet: Illustrated Timeline by Junipero Serra's life extending from his birth through his death and subsequent recognition and beatification; 2005 Pentacle Press.

Memo from professor at Fresno Pacific College to manager of the gift shop at Carmel Mission Basilica (n.d.).

Pamphlet: "The Mass and Dedication of the Harry Downie Museum."

Monterey Peninsula Herald, July 21, 1974, "Swinging Ringers Ring Mission Bells."

Monterey Peninsula Herald (n.d.), "New Carmel Mission Chapel Completed."

The Herald, September 21, 2009, "Wooden Cross at Beach Cut Down."

The Herald, Monday, May 16, 2011, *"Hotel Wasn't Luxury for Pilot Trainees."*

San Luis Obispo Telegram-Tribune (n.d.), "Renovations of the Mission have revealed many things."

San Luis Obispo Telegram-Tribune" (n.d.), "Restoration offers clues about Mission – at one time adobe walls were painted red."

Monterey Peninsula Herald, Thursday, July 13, 1950, "Bing Starts the Ball Rolling . . . New Carmel Mission Launched."

Monterey Peninsula Herald, Monday, February 8, 1954, "70,000 Catholic Pilgrims to Converge on Carmel Mission in May."

Monterey Peninsula Herald, January 13, 1955, "750 Attend Dinner Honoring Carmel Mission Restorer."

The Herald Weekend Magazine, September 16, 1972, "Art Treasures Get Loving Care at Carmel Mission."

The Sunday Peninsula Herald, October 12, 1980, "Museums in Carmel Mission Basilica Garden Opens."

Monterey Peninsula Herald, Wednesday, January 11, 1984, "Citizens Act Without Officials Permission," "Redwood Cross Returns to Carmel Meadows Area."

Athanasius Schaefer, "San Carlos de Borromeo de Carmelo," http//www.athanasius.com/camission/carmel.htm, 11-5-2010

The Herald, Thursday, January 5, 2012, "Archaeologist Aids Stamp Design."

Cassette Tape. Side A. Harry Downie, Recollections of the restoration of Mission Soledad. Side B. Harry Downie, Recollections of the restoration of Mission San Juan Bautista.

Spanish Missions in California, from Wikipedia the free encyclopedia, 01-17-2013.

The Herald, Wednesday, December 25, 2013, "Looking Back on a Special Mission."

The Sunday Herald, Sunday, January 25, 2009, "Restoration Prescription."

The Herald (n.d.), "Beach Cross to be replaced, Council decides."

The Herald, March 2, 2010, "Controversial Cross to Stand in Cemetery."

The Herald, Friday, April 16, 2010, "Ringing in a new era for mission."

Booklet: "The Story of the Father Junipero Serra Memorial Cenotaph."

The Monterey Californian, "San Carlos Day," "A Barbarian at the Carmello Mission," November 11, 1879.

Noticias del Puerto de Monterey, A Quarterly Bulletin of Historic Monterey Issued by the Monterey History and Art Association, Vol. XXV, No. 1, March 1982. REBUILDER OF MISSIONS: Henry John "Harry" Downie 1903–1980.

California Information Almanac, Past Present Future, Prepared and Published by Edward V. Salitore, President and Publisher, P.O. Box 400, Lakewood, California 90714, 1973.

Pamphlet, Mission Bell, Campaign for the Preservation of Mission San Antonio de Padua, Vol. 3, No. 2/Summer 2014.

Eugene W. Biscailuz – from Wikipedia, the free encyclopedia, 7-28-14.

Monterey Herald, Friday, January 16, 2015, "Pope plans to Canonize Fr. Serra."

Cornerstone, Newsletter of the Carmel Mission Foundation, Fall 2011.

The Argonaut, Vol. III, No. 16, San Francisco, October 26, 1878.

Alta Vista Magazine, Sunday, January 22, 1995, "San Carlos Cathedral and the birthday nobody noticed."

The Sunday Peninsula Herald Weekend Magazine, August 26, 1984, "Junipero Serra – 1713–1784"

Ibid, "Portola's Misfortunate Journey."

Ibid, "Serra's Arduous Path to Sainthood."

San Francisco Chronicle, Monday, September 5, 1988, "The Legacy of Father Serra's Missions."

San Diego Gazette, April 15 to May 15, 1993, "The Missions of California."

Catenary Arch, from Wikipedia, the free encyclopedia, 8-15-2017.

Salinas Californian, Valley Today, Tuesday, June 3, 1980, "Downie's Aide Takes Over," Linda Lewis.

INDEX

A

Abluton, Bruno, 11
Academy of Franciscan
  History, 83
Adenauer, Konrad, 4
Alaska, 20
Aleutian Islands, 20
Alfonso, King XIII of
  Spain, 49
Arguello, Louis Antonio, 7
Armstrong, Rev. Robert, 43

B

Barcelos, Rui, 61
Bartholomew, Saint, 25
Blessed Sacrament
  Chapel, 54
Bonaparte, Napoleon, 68
Borgel and Downie, 7
Bouchard, Hippolyte de, 27
Brother Benedict, 75

C

California Historical
  Society, 103
Carmelite Monastery, 60
Carmelite Padres, 25
Casanova, Fr. Angelo, 2, 14, 55
Charles III, King, 25
Clinch, Harry A. Bishop, 87
Colton Hall, 81
Colton, Walter, 2
Conover, Elbert M., 84
Crespi, Fr. Juan, 16, 22, 23
Crosby, Bing, 54
Culleton, Msgr. James, 15, 18
Currivan, Earl and
  Margaret, 12

D

Daly, Patrick, Msgr., 72

Dana, Richard Henry, Jr., 70
de Cortona, Margarita, 75
de Galvez, Jose, 34
de Gama, Vasco, 35
de Haro, Francisco, 7
de Matute, Juan Bautista, 37
Dockweiler, I. B. Senator, 47
Dollar Steamship Lines, 4
Dominican Convent, 16
Durein, Ted, 84

E
Earthquakes
  1812, 41
  1906, 7, 8
Eisenhower, Dwight, 4

F
Farrell, Lawrence, 4, 5, 107, 108
Ferdinand, King VII of Spain, 68
Field, Maria, 49
Fort Ross, 68, 69
Foss, Kristina, 18, 19
Francisca, Sister, 59–61
Franco, Francisco, General, 83

Fresno Pacific University, 86

G
Gaspar, 4, 12, 62
Gateway Arch, 26
Geiger, Fr. Maynard J., 82
Gomez, Andrew, 40
Greely, Horace, 55

H
Hart, Mrs., 55
Hathaway, Pat, 64
Hearst Castle, 10, 81
Hearst Foundation, 71, 74
Hobrecht, Fr. Augustine, 49
Hunt, A. T. Cabinet Firm, 10

I
Influenza epidemic, 9, 10

J
Jackson, Helen Hunt, 2, 6, 80
Jayme, Fr. Luis, 18, 22
Jesuit Novitiate, 4
Jo Mora Chapel, 16, 17
John, XXIII, Pope, 56
John Paul II, Pope, 57

Junipero Serra School, 53

K
Kennedy, John F.,
  President, 4, 47

L
Laiolo, Barney, 105
La Playa Hotel, 60
Lasuen, Fr. Fermin, 16, 25, 78
Life Magazine, 49
Lombardo, Nick, 102
Lopez, Fr. Julien, 16
Los Gatos, 4
Los Osos, 22

M
Manning, Timothy,
  Archbishop, 103
Margaret, Princess,
  Great Britain, 4
Marion, George, 13
McEldowney, Joe, 14
McGucken, Bishop,
  Joseph, 71
McMenamin, Fr. George, 87
Mellon, Knox, 88
Mendoza, Ruben, 88
Menn, Richard, 64
Morrison, Rose, 7
Mortons, 64–66
Mortuary Chapel, 38, 39

N
National Guard, 76
Naval Postgraduate
  School, 66, 84
Nguyen, Huu Van, 62, 63
Nietzsche, Friedrich
  Wilhelm, 105

O
O'Boyle, Emmett, 6, 64
O'Connell, Rev. Michael, 72, 88
Odello, Bruna, 12
Odello, Emilio, 11, 12, 87
Our Lady of
  Bethlehem, 33–37

P
Padres' library, 43–44
Pala, San Antonio de, 67
Palos Colorados, 31
Palou, Fr. Francisco, 8

Panetta, Leon,
Congressman, 50, 103, 104
Pious Fund, 68
Plaza Church, 81
Pope Pius VI, 18
Pope Pius XII, 83
Portola, Gaspar de, 21–23, 29–31
Poschen, Edward, 39

R
Reagan, Ronald, 44
Real, Fr. Jose Maria, 55
Reinecke, Ed, Lt. Gov., 31
Reredos, 55, 56
Rodriguez, Msgr. Amancio, 79
Royal Presidio Chapel, 27
Rubio, Fr., 79
Ruiz, Esteban, 27
Ruiz, Juan Maria, 75
Ryan, Msgr. John, 15

S
Sacred Expedition, 21, 34
San Carlos Church, 4, 8, 13, 14, 22
San Francisco Bay, 22
Santa Barbara, 4
Scher, Msgr., Philip, 5
Secularization, 67
Serra, Fr. Junipero, 1, 2, 10, 11, 13–18, 20–22, 26, 29, 34, 36, 37, 40–44, 47–49, 56, 60, 64, 70–73, 93, 95
Shanley, Brian, 87, 88
Shelley, John, Mayor S.F., 84
Ships:
San Antonio, 21, 23
San Carlos, 21
San Jose, 21
Silveira, Gregorio, 72
Sister Serra, 16
Sisters of Notre Dame, 53
Sitjar, Fr. Buenaventura, 75
Soberanes, Edward, 62
Stevenson, Robert Louis, 3
Sullivan, Fr. John, 9
Sunset Books, 42
Sutter, Ann, 54

T
Taylor, Bayard, 55
TIME magazine, 49

Treaty of Cordoba, 69

U
Udall, Stewart L., 4

V
Vera Cruz, 46

Vigilance, Committee of, 7
Vizcaino, 22, 25

W
Weber, Msgr. Francis J., 82
Willinger, Bishop Aloysius J., 55

Made in the USA
Las Vegas, NV
20 September 2023